PROMISE DEFERRED

To Bob Fisher for your kindness shown to a stranger, gratefully

the Author

Siegfried Horn

Pleasant Hill, Oct. 21, 1988

PROMISE DEFERRED

Siegfried H. Horn

REVIEW AND HERALD PUBLISHING ASSOCIATION
Washington, DC 20039-0555
Hagerstown, MD 21740

Copyright © 1987 by
Review and Herald Publishing Association

This book was
Edited by Gerald Wheeler
Book design and cover art by Richard Steadham
Type set: 11/12 Bookman

Printed in U.S.A.

Bible texts credited to RSV are from the Revised Standard Version, copyrighted 1946, 1952 © 1971, 1973.

Library of Congress Cataloging in Publication Data

Horn, Siegfried H., 1908-
  Promise deferred.

    1. Horn, Siegfried H., 1908-   . 2. World War, 1939-1945—Prisoners and prisons, Dutch. 3.World War, 1939-1945—Personal narratives, German. 4. Prisoners of war—Indonesia—Biography. 5. Prisoners of war—India—Biography. 6. Prisoners of war—Germany—Biography. 7. Missionaries—Indonesia—Biography. I. Title.
D805.I55H67   1987   940.54'72'43   87-4593

ISBN   0-8280-0380-7

Contents

Preface		7
Introduction		9
I	Overnight From Missionary to Prisoner	15
II	From Despair to Hope	23
III	In the Jungles of Sumatra	34
IV	A Prisoner's Life of Study	44
V	Saved From Death by Mistake	52
VI	In India: East, West, and North	66
VII	Free at Last	82
VIII	Epilogue	93

Preface

In the fall of 1946, more than a year after the end of World War II, I and nine other Seventh-day Adventist missionaries arrived in the United States from a six-and-one-half-year internment. During the preceding year many soldiers and civilians, who had spent terrible periods of incarceration in Japanese or German prison camps, had received warm welcomes in their homeland and had related their adventures. Among them had been scores of Adventist missionaries who had served their church in the Far East and elsewhere. We, however, were a novelty, because we were Germans who had been held in custody by the Allies in Asia. Few Americans had ever met such former prisoners or heard their stories.

It was for this reason that as soon as I arrived in America I had invitations to tell my experiences in numerous churches, schools, and civic clubs from coast to coast. These requests have continued to the present day, 40 years after my imprisonment ended. Innumerable times I have been asked to publish my war experiences. I always declined this since I felt that I needed to use my time to write on more important subject matter.

It was only during a recent two-month stint of teaching in the Seventh-day Adventist Theological Seminary, Far East, that I finally decided to give in to these frequently lodged requests to publish the story of God's marvelous dealings with me during World War II. The organizers of the seminary's annual faculty and staff retreat requested that I tell my story in segments like chapters of a book. I did so during a nature walk on a Sabbath afternoon and around an open camp fire later in the evening in the wonderful mountain world of Luzon in the Philippines. After I finished my last talk someone again asked me to write them down and publish them, because with my advancing age, the opportunity could soon vanish.

Just at that time I received an unscheduled vacation when the Philippine government under President Marcos closed all schools for two weeks. He did this to get the restless students away from their campuses during the most critical days preceding the presidential election that led to the well-known four-day revolution that toppled Marcos and brought in Corazon Aquino as the new president. I used the time to compose the first draft of this little book. After my return to America I put the finishing touches on it and supplied dates and certain other facts to the manuscript with the help of my war diary, which I had been able to smuggle from one camp to another and finally bring with me to the United States.

The purpose of this book is to show that even behind the most discouraging events there may be discernible—often only much later on—the guiding hand of God. My own war experiences have demonstrated that this has certainly been true in my life. It is my hope and prayer that my story will persuade many readers to accept God's will for their life even if it is not always easy to see His leading hand during painful times.

The Author

Introduction

The story recounted in this book is one of the best I have ever heard. It belongs to one of the most remarkable men I have ever met—a renowned archaeologist, noted professor, prolific author, esteemed churchman, and fast friend.

Because many readers may not realize that the experience Siegfried Horn relates here represents only a few years in the life of an influential scholar, it may be useful to set those years in the context of his career, which has lasted three quarters of a century.

Siegfried Herbert Horn was born in Wurzen, Germany, on March 17, 1908, the son of one of the world's first aviators. He received his undergraduate education at Friedensau Seminary (Germany) in 1926 to 1928, and then at Stanborough College (England) from 1929 to 1930. His subsequent active professional life was divided in two unequal parts by the years of internment as a prisoner of war— a story that is told so well in this book. Before that six-and-a-half-year interlude, Horn served from 1930 to 1940 as a minister in the Netherlands and a missionary teacher/administrator in the Dutch East Indies. During his internment—and indeed, his whole life—it can be said of him as it was of the Holy Land's early explorer, Edward Robinson: "He used freely whatever lay open to be freely used. But he took the learning of others, whether dead or living, not for a Jacob's pillow to sleep on, but for a Jacob's ladder to climb by" (quoted in F. J. Bliss, *The Development of Palestine Exploration,* p. 203).

Upon gaining his freedom, Horn immigrated to the United States and quickly completed his formal education with a B.A. from Walla Walla College (Washington), 1946-1947, an M.A. from the SDA Theological Seminary (Washington, D.C.), 1947-1948, with a thesis entitled "The Topographical History of Palestine According to the Egyptian Asiatic Lists and Other Sources,'' and a Ph.D. from the University of Chicago, 1948-1951, with a thesis ''The Relation Between Egypt and Asia During the Egyptian Middle Kingdom.'' From 1951 to 1976 Horn taught at Andrews University (in Berrien Springs, Michigan), from which he retired as professor emeritus of archaeology and history of antiquity. Even in retirement he has remained active in writing, traveling, and lecturing. As I write, he is in Jerusalem for several months directing the academic program at the newly established Jerusalem Center for Biblical and Archaeological Studies.

As an archaeologist, Horn was not satisfied in merely utilizing the results of others' archaeological fieldwork. He wanted to make his own contribution. In the early 1960s he joined the staff of the Tell Balatah (biblical Shechem) expedition. That experience only whetted his appetite for his own ''dig,'' which he carefully planned and subsequently fielded at Tell Hesban (biblical Heshbon) in 1968, 1971, and 1973. He continued with the project as senior adviser and object registrar in 1974 and 1976. These excavations became the largest in the country of Jordan and the training ground for numerous national and foreign archaeologists. Heshbon soon became noted for its superb organization, its quality methods, and the prompt preliminary publication of its results. In 1970 Horn founded the archaeological museum at Andrews University that now bears his name. The next year, 1970-1971, he served as director of the American Center of Oriental Research in Amman, Jordan. An indication of the esteem in which archaeological circles hold him is the fact that some 200 scholars gathered in Atlanta, Georgia, in November 1986 for the surprise presentation to him of a book of essays in his honor, *The Archaeology of Jordan and Other Studies Presented to Siegfried H. Horn*. Published by Andrews University Press, the volume contains contributions by some 30 leading archaeologists and biblical scholars from around the world.

As a professor, Horn established a reputation for giving students their money's worth in such courses as Archaeology and the Bible, Old Testament Backgrounds, and Introduction to the Old Testament. He was a master of the material he presented. And it was always current, thanks to his own personal library, which contains thousands of archaeological and biblical volumes and outshines, in those areas, most college libraries. He stayed on top of discoveries through his membership in numerous scholarly and professional organizations, including the Palestine Exploration Fund, Palestine Oriental Society, German Palestine Society, American Oriental Society, American Schools of Oriental Research, Society of Biblical Literature, and the Chicago Society of Biblical Research (of which he served as president). He began the doctoral program at Andrews University. Not content with the classroom alone, he led several renowned study tours to the Middle East. By this means, he encouraged scores of denominational teachers, pastors, evangelists, and editors to incorporate into their ministries firsthand knowledge of the historical and geographical context of the biblical drama.

As an author, few are his equal. Horn has written nearly 800 articles and several books. In fact, he authored half the articles on biblical archaeology to appear in denominational journals over a 30-year period. His employment of archeological evidence had three major goals: to show how a knowledge of the ancient world makes the Bible more meaningful; to substantiate faith in the Bible by demonstrating the veracity of its historical statements; and to demonstrate the faithful transmission of the biblical text, so no one need doubt what the biblical author intended to say. From the beginning, Horn participated in the production of the multivolume *Seventh-day Adventist Bible Commentary*. In addition to reading it all in manuscript and galley form, he himself authored 963 pages of articles and exegesis in the printed work. Perhaps Horn's single most influential book is his *Seventh-day Adventist Bible Dictionary* (a part of the Review and Herald's Commentary Reference Series), which is now in a revised edition. Among one-volume Bible dictionaries on the market, it has been characterized as the most reliable and best informed on archaeology.

Not only did Horn himself write; he encouraged others to do the same. In 1963 he founded *Andrews University Seminary Studies,* the denomination's first scholarly periodical whose articles are now indexed, abstracted, or listed in at least 15 scholarly sources. Shortly thereafter he inaugurated *Andrews University Monographs: Studies in Religion* for book-length manuscripts.

As a churchman, Horn has brought balance into a communion sometimes tempted to extremes. He has served his denomination, at one time or another, on every continent, as pastor, missionary, teacher, editor, committeeman, curator, and seminary dean, choosing to make his major contributions within and for the benefit of the church. He has left his imprint on Adventism—both in terms of scholarly method and commonly accepted truth. And his centrist legacy lives on in the lives and careers of the numerous pastors, teachers, and scholars he has influenced and inspired.

As one considers the many lives of Siegfried Horn, those of us who have known him well can testify personally that this man, for all his learning and for all his rather formal Prussian exterior, is a warm, enthusiastic man—an individual whom we are proud to call a friend.

I first met Horn in 1947, exactly 40 years ago, when as a 7-year-old child I lived in the same apartment building in Takoma Park, Maryland, as he and his wife. My father and he were taking classes at the SDA Theological Seminary at the time, Horn having just gotten out of internment camp and completed his bachelor's degree at Walla Walla College, and my father being on furlough from mission service behind Japanese lines in China during World War II. My recollection of him was that he was a very businesslike neighbor. The next time we met was in Beirut, Lebanon, in 1953. He was on his first trip to the Holy Land, and by this time my parents had moved from the Far East to the Middle East, where my father served as president of Middle East College. As a teenager I was fascinated with Horn's account of the discovery of the Dead Sea scrolls and their significance for the Bible. On another of his trips to the Middle East, in 1959, he graciously allowed my brother and me to join his tour to Egypt and Israel, where for the first time we came face-to-face with sites and sights so pertinent to the biblical account. It was during those years that I gained my interest and love for archaeology, ancient history, and the Bible. Eventually, I ended up at the SDA Theological Seminary at Andrews University, where as a student I took all the courses that Horn offered. Little did I expect that after I had served as a pastor and pursued my own doctoral program at Harvard, Siegfried Horn would choose me to succeed him at Andrews teaching archaeology, directing his dig in Jordan, and curating in the museum that is now a part of the Institute of

Archaeology at Andrews University. I will always be grateful for his mentoring and confidence.

On several occasions over the years I have been privileged to hear firsthand the story related in this book. I have never tired of it. Apart from its being fascinating as a story, it has much to commend it. From a divine perspective, it is encouraging to see Providence at work. From the human perspective, it is inspiring to see how a person of faith can move beyond circumstances that would daunt most, even making those very circumstances work in his favor. From a theological point of view, the reader finds himself confronted in the story with difficult ethical dilemmas—one can learn by looking over Horn's shoulder. From a practical point of view, one learns history, geography, sociology, and science from a keen observer/chronicler of every aspect of life.

I trust that the readers of this account will be influenced by the example of Siegfried Horn to make the most of their own trying and difficult circumstances, so that they too may make such apparent barriers veritable pathways to success for themselves and blessings for countless others. If that happens, and I know it will, the retelling of the story in its published form will not have been in vain.

                    Lawrence T. Geraty
                    President and Professor of Archaeology
                    Atlantic Union College
                    South Lancaster, Massachusetts

March 17, 1987
(Siegfried Horn's seventy-ninth birthday)

Chapter I

Overnight From Missionary to Prisoner

During a warm, muggy Friday night in the spring of 1940 I returned on my faithful Harley-Davidson motorcycle to my home in old Batavia, now Djakarta. Entering the house from the rear I heard the call Sepada—the general Indonesian term used to notify a resident of the arrival of a visitor. Going to the front door I faced two police officers who took me into custody. An imprisonment began that would last for nearly six and a half years and would take me thousands of miles over land and sea to five internment camps before it all ended in far-off India. The first camp was on a small island, the next in the midst of an impenetrable jungle, after that the camps were in two barren deserts, and finally in the lovely foothills of the Himalayas, the highest mountains on earth.

World War II had broken out in the autumn of 1939 when Nazi Germany's forces invaded Poland and captured and occupied that unhappy land in collusion with Soviet Russia. France and Britain at once declared war against Germany in order to honor their treaty obligations toward Poland. They also tried belatedly to stop Hitler's insatiable hunger for the territories of his smaller neighbor nations. However, land hostilities on any measurable scale did not break out between the belligerent powers during the remaining months of 1939 nor during the first three months of 1940. But in early April 1940 exciting events began to happen when Germany occupied in one stroke defenseless Denmark and invaded and conquered peaceful Norway in short order. One month later, on Friday, May 10, 1940, the long-expected struggle between the great powers began when Germany attacked the French-British forces through neutral Belgium. On the same day the German forces invaded the small country of the Netherlands, which had also wanted to remain neutral. The Netherlands surrendered five days later after air raids had largely destroyed its second-largest city, Rotterdam. Belgium continued to fight on for another two weeks, and France held out until the middle of June before being invaded. However, Britain's forces escaped annihilation and capture by evacuating via Dunkirk. This is in a nutshell the historical background of what happened before and immediately after my fateful May day.

I had been a German missionary in what had been for about 300 years a Dutch colonial empire, the Netherlands East Indies. It consisted of thousands of islands that stretched from central New Guinea in the east to the northern tip of Sumatra in the west, a distance of 3,100 miles, a distance approximately equal to that from New York to San Francisco. These islands, straddling the equator between Asia and Australia, were home to about 70 million Indonesians of many colorful tribes and possessed rich natural resources such as tin and oil as well as such tropical products as tea, coffee, sugar, spices, timber, and rice.

For nearly eight happy years I had served the Seventh-day Adventist churches and schools of Java and Sumatra as pastor and administrator in many capacities during the trying and difficult years of the Great Depression. My work had been immensely interesting and most satisfying, and my travels through plantations and tropical jungles, mountainous areas and fertile plains, had always been enjoyable.

During those eight years I had lived twice in Djakarta, the capital of the country, for a total of six years. Sandwiched between the two Djakarta sojourns I spent two years in Semarang, Central Java. Because of the shortage of missionaries during my second Djakarta term I worked not only in the West Java Mission Field but was also administrator and the only ordained minister of the South Sumatra Mission. The latter reached from the southern tip of the island—Tanjung Karang—to the oil fields of Palembang on the east coast and to Benghulu on the west coast. During nine extended trips to Sumatra I thus became well acquainted with its land and people.

Among the high points of those years I must place my ordination to the gospel ministry and my wedding to Jeanne Rothfusz, a nurse from Delft in Holland, with whom I had become acquainted during a two-and-one-half-year stay in the Netherlands prior to my arrival in the East Indies. The reason that we could not get married before

I left for Java in 1932 was again the Great Depression. Since the Mission Board was so short of money at that time, it could send only one new missionary out in a given year. Hence I went out in 1932 and my fiancée a year later. However, the Java years were not only filled with joy and exhilarating experiences; they were also tinged with sadness. We lost our only child, a son, in 1939. It put a drop of bitter gall into the happiness that usually had filled the cup of our lives.

My interesting and satisfying life as a missionary came to a rude and sudden end on Friday, May 10, 1940, when Hitler sent Germany's armed forces into Holland. Suddenly I became an enemy alien in the country I had lived in for almost eight years, and at once it treated me as such.

On that fateful Friday I returned at noon by train from an extended trip during which I had visited isolated members of the Dutch church in Djakarta who were employed on plantations in various parts of western Java. I was just about ready to begin the customary afternoon siesta when I heard through our open window the neighbor's radio advising its listeners that an important announcement was to be broadcast. At once I turned our radio on and heard the governor general of the Netherlands East Indies informing the nation that Hitler's Germany had begun an invasion of the motherland that very day. He therefore proclaimed the existence of a state of war between the Netherlands East Indies and Germany, mentioning also that the authorities had either already interned all German citizens or would arrest them as soon as they could locate them.

The news hit me like a thunderclap. My mouth became so dry that I could hardly speak to my wife or answer the phone, which began to ring incessantly, since concerned church members wanted to know what would happen to me. I drank innumerable glasses of water to quench my thirst and calm down. By sundown I had become somewhat relaxed. Then I dressed and drove my motorcycle to church where I presented my weekly public lecture in Dutch, fearing that it might be the last one for a long time. Yet I did not think at that time—not even in my wildest expectations—that six and a half years would pass before I would once more stand as a free man in front of a congregation. After my lecture I had a meeting with the officers of the church and discussed with them the measures they should take if I would not be able to come to church the next day, which was Sabbath.

Having done this I returned home, whereupon I was arrested, as I have already related. The officers who took me into custody permitted me to pack a suitcase into which I put some clothing and underwear, a small pocket-size Dutch Bible, and—I do not know why—a one-volume Bible dictionary. Not being a prophet, I could not foresee that exactly 20 years later the *Seventh-day Adventist Bible Dictionary,* of which I would be the principal author, would come off the press.

The ride to the local police station was short. There I found myself joining a large group of Djakarta's German residents, some of whom had lived there for many years. A little later Jeanne arrived with one of our church members and brought me some sandwiches so that I would have something to eat the next day. They had correctly guessed that it would be a long time before the authorities would feed us. When I once more said goodbye to Jeanne and kissed her, we did not know that seven years would pass before we would meet again, that I—and she also—would go through trying and cruel experiences before she would serve me another meal. A merciful Providence put a veil in front of our future. It was hard to leave her behind in a foreign country where she had no relatives to help her, while her homeland, where her father, brothers, and sisters lived, underwent a baptism of fire as never before.

A couple of hours later several garbage trucks arrived at the police station. At once we suspected that they had come to pick us up. We received orders to climb on the infernal smelling vehicles. Most of us wore clean, starched, and well pressed white suits as European or American businessmen or officials customarily dressed in the East Indies. Someone in higher circles must have thought of this deeply humiliating gesture to make us realize right from the outset that we no longer were part of the civilized and honor- or respect-deserving section of the human race, but, as a newspaper in those days expressed it, could only be compared with "Huns and cave hyenas."

As our rumbling trucks drove us at midnight through the dark streets of peacefully sleeping Djakarta toward the harbor of Tanjung

Priok it was hard to realize that the only thing changed in this city, in which I had lived as a respected resident for years, was the status of us Germans.

When we reached the harbor, the police herded us into a large godown (warehouse) where they had already gathered hundreds of other arrested Germans. I met some men whom I knew: a rather well-known doctor, a highly respected bank director, several successful businessmen, and others with whom I had become acquainted during the annual Ingathering Campaigns when we missionaries visited them and asked them to support our philanthropic work. Many, who had arrived at the godown hours before we came, had already bedded down on the naked cement floor, so that we latecomers had a hard time finding unoccupied spots to rest.

The worst was to come. The only toilet the warehouse possessed proved to be far from adequate to serve the needs of hundreds of men, and the total absence of any water in a building intended to store dry goods, not living human beings, made the next morning even more trying. The building had a roof of corrugated iron sheets on which the sun beat down unmercifully and made our situation even more uncomfortable. It was, therefore, a great relief when during the afternoon the authorities brought several empty barrels in to supplement the one existing toilet, canisters with drinking water, and some large kettles with steaming rice and dry salt fish. Although most people had not eaten for the last 24 hours, they were not yet hungry enough to eat a bowl of hot rice with salt fish. Hardly anyone touched this lavish meal. The only other thing I remember of that first and oh so long day of my imprisonment was the arrival of new prisoners from time to time. They came from different parts of western Java and usually received a noisy and enthusiastic welcome from friends who knew them.

Although the conditions in which we spent that first day were extremely primitive, I noticed that the atmosphere was one of cheerfulness and high expectations. Reminding each other that Germany had defeated Poland in a few weeks and overpowered Denmark and Norway in a matter of days, we all expected that the campaign against the Netherlands would require only a few days. One of the conditions of the expected ceasefire would unquestionably be our release by the Dutch colonial government. When that

19

time would come, we could take revenge for the shabby treatment we were getting. Although we were right in expecting the military campaign against the Dutch motherland to be a short one, we certainly were far off the mark in thinking that it would change our situation.

In the late afternoon an officer appeared flanked by several armed soldiers. He told us to get ready for our departure. When we passed through the open door, we found the space in front of our godown surrounded by native soldiers with their rifles at the ready. At a distance scores of harbor coolies squatted, watching in amazement as the white *tuhans* (masters) carried their own luggage—something they had never witnessed before—and received harsh orders from Dutch Army officers. The wildest coolie dream seemed to have come true.

Surrounded by soldiers from all sides we marched to a pier where a waiting freighter received us in its holds. As I climbed down a steep stairway into one of the holds, I ran into Andy Krautschick, one of my fellow missionaries, who had lived and worked in Bandung, one of Java's pleasant hill cities, which enjoys a year-round temperate climate. In the semi-darkness of the hold I also saw a large group of half-naked and extremely dirty and greasy men. They turned out to be the crew members from several German ships. Since the sailors had received no warning of any kind that a war between Germany and the Netherlands had broken out, military commandos were able to overrun their ships before they had had an opportunity to scuttle them. The reason they had been in the dark about what happened in the world was because the Dutch authorities had removed all their wireless equipment and radios when they sought refuge in the harbors of the East Indies. The sailors, unaware of what had happened in Europe, had therefore easily been overpowered and been taken from their ships just as they were. They had been scraping off old paint from steel walls, painting, or doing repair work and other related jobs. Most of them wore little more than shorts and sandals and would have nothing else for several weeks.

Although our voyage from the harbor of Tanjung Priok to our destination was a short one and lasted only two hours, it was a hellish experience. Many hundreds of men were packed in the holds below deck, with no ventilation. Soon we could understand how the people in the Black Hole of Calcutta must have felt before they suffocated. When the ship's engines stopped and the crew removed the covering of the holds, all of the internees tried to get out as quickly as possible. The young, strong sailors fought their way out first with brutal strength, while those of us with suitcases had to wait longer for relief.

It took some time to get all prisoners out of the holds since the Dutch colonial authorities had only one motorboat available to pull a barge to ferry us from the ship to the nearby island. When I thought I could no longer stand the thick, foul air, I tried working my way to the stairs. My suitcase, however, acted like a drag anchor. At one point my right arm with my suitcase remained wedged in between some men pushing in another direction. I feared they would tear my arm from my body. Soaked in perspiration, I eventually made the deck and could breathe the refreshing night air of the Java Sea. I felt as if I had escaped from a tomb and was resurrected to a new life.

Another disappointment came when we reached shore. There we received orders to leave all our luggage on an open field. I said goodbye to all the earthly goods that I possessed at that moment, and expected never to see them again. After the experiences of the previous day I began to question whether we would meet another decent man among the people with whom I had happily worked for many years and whom I had highly respected, but who had suddenly turned into bitter enemies. My belief in the innate goodness of the human soul had received a big jolt and was rapidly disappearing.

Now they directed us to line up two abreast and then marched us through pitch-dark alleys lined by barbed-wire fences that we could faintly see by means of the weak beams of electric flashlights carried by the native soldiers who accompanied us. An officer opened the gate of one enclosure after another, each time separating 110 internees from the rest, letting them in, and locking the enclosure behind him.

We tried to find out what kind of accommodations the Dutch government had provided for us. First I learned from someone who seemed to be in the know that we had landed on the small island of Onrust—the name means "no rest"—which was one of the Thousand Islands in the Bay of Djakarta. I also found out that the authorities generally used the island as a quarantine station to screen passengers who returned from a voyage to Mecca, the pilgrimage every faithful Moslem wants to make once during his life.

The barbed-wire enclosures existing on the island for that purpose seemed to the authorities to be well suited to serve as a temporary internment camp until they could construct more permanent facilities elsewhere. However, the results of our cursory inspection in utter darkness were not too promising. We saw that our enclosure contained a long metal shed resting on a cement floor. It was completely empty. In front of the shed stood two large trees, while a small metal structure in one corner of the enclosure seemed to be an outhouse.

Since most prisoners had hardly had anything to eat and little to drink during the last day and a half, all were extremely hungry and thirsty. Finding neither water nor food, the enraged men screamed in unison: "We want water! We want food!" The inmates of the other areas joined the shouting. Soon it seemed that the officials in faraway Djakarta could not help hearing us. However, nothing happened. When the futility of all our screaming finally sunk in, the shouting eventually died down. One after another we sank to the cement floor inside the sheds or on the sand or grass outside and tried to get some sleep. It was the second night in a row that I had slept on cement.

Only a little more than a day had passed since my arrest, the first of more than 2,290 days to follow, but I already thought that I had had enough! I began to have some sympathy with those people who cursed our tormentors. What would happen next? Would I be a despised and humiliated prisoner the rest of my life? The questions raced through my mind until a light sleep gave me some relief for a few blessed hours.

Chapter II

From Despair to Hope

It was already light when I woke up on Sunday morning. I was stiff, and my bones and muscles ached from sleeping on the hard cement. The sun beat down on us from a cloudless sky. The little tropical island would be our home for the next two months.

Another brutal and long day began. The worst thing was that we still had nothing to drink. We discovered an iron pipe sticking out of the ground, but no water issued from it. Eventually we learned that the island had no natural water source at all, and that all water had to be transported to it from the mainland. The first water tanker did not arrive until noon. Also the toilet facilities consisted of nothing more than some holes in the ground surrounded by a sheet metal contraption.

Yet, in the course of the day the first phases of an organization went into action. Eventually Indonesian soldiers distributed drinking water. Workmen repaired the electric wires so that the alleyways between the barbed-wire fences could be illuminated at night. They also installed a shower head on the pipe that would bring us water for half an hour twice every day so that we could take showers and rinse our underwear. And the latrines got some wooden boards on which the prisoners could squat or sit. Each inmate received a metal plate and spoon and every enclosure got several empty tin cans which the prisoners had to share. They had to serve as drinking cups until the authorities could import drinking utensils for us from the mainland a few days later. Before the day was out we obtained our first meal. Life began to appear less hopeless at day's end than it had looked in the morning.

Nevertheless, it was a most primitive existence. The only clothes we had were what we had worn when we entered the camp. Since we had no soap to wash, most of us stripped down to our underwear and ran around like that as long as we remained in the island camp. We had no toothbrushes to brush our teeth or scissors to cut fingernails or trim hair, no razors to shave or towels to dry ourselves after the daily short rinse, no mosquito nets to protect us from the malaria-carrying mosquitoes, no pens to write with, and no books, magazines, or newspapers to read.

In fact, we considered the complete lack of newspapers as one of the most severe punishments. During those days when some of the most earthshaking events took place, and some of the most historic battles of all times altered the political map of Europe, we were completely isolated from any news. Instead of receiving reliable news, all kinds of rumors circulated, but we never knew what was true and what was false. Only several weeks after our internment started did I see parts of a newspaper for the first time. The pages had somehow been smuggled into our camp and made their way from one cage to the next. They gave us glimpses of what the real situation in the world was. Eagerly we ate up every word of this news, since it offered us some reliable information of what was really happening in the outside world.

On the second or third day of our internment an officer announced the camp regulations. He came to the gate of our enclosure in full dress with white gloves on his hands and pompously read them to us. They bristled with words such as "do not," "forbidden," and "prohibited," and were generously peppered with threatened punishments for violations, of which the terms "will be shot," "executed," or "fusilladed" played the most prominent roles. That they were not hollow threats we discovered a few hours later.

Suddenly a shot rang out, and a man in the enclosure next to ours slumped to the ground. He had touched one of the barbed-wire fences, probably without remembering that touching it violated the new rules. One of the soldiers who stood at every crosspoint of the alleyways must have seen it and at once fired without any warning. At the crack of the rifle several Dutch Army officers with drawn revolvers raced to the enclosure where the wounded man lay on the ground, and ordered all inmates of that cage as well as of the adjacent ones, mine included, to get into their sheds and stay there until we received permission to come out. When some medics entered the enclosure with a stretcher, the man had already bled to death. After this terrifying event we carefully read and reread the camp regulations—now issued in written form—to know what we could and could not do.

Soon we witnessed another scary event. Professor Thierfelder, who before his arrest had headed the Institute Pasteur in Bandung, and who had been decorated by Queen Wilhelmina of the Netherlands for his meritorious work in combating the plague in the Indies, was an internee in an adjacent enclosure. His fellow inmates chose him to be their leader and spokesman. Such a leader was responsible to keep order, take care of the food distribution at the mealtimes, and serve as liaison with the authorities. The only one allowed to address any officer who would daily come to receive reports about cases of sickness, he also provided men to help in the kitchen, unload the ships that arrived every day to bring us our water and food from the mainland, or for other corvée duties.

One day Professor Thierfelder mentioned to the liaison officer that the morale in his enclosure would materially improve if his men could only get some soap and cigarettes. The Dutch officer reported his remark to the camp commandant, who thereupon came personally to Thierfelder's enclosure with a small detachment of soldiers. He called Thierfelder out of his enclosure and ordered his fellow prisoners to elect another leader. Then he commanded Thierfelder to kneel down to be chained by the wrists and ankles, after which he announced that the professor would be executed for having incited his fellow internees to rebel. He was led away, and we heard nothing more about him for about a week, after which we saw Thierfelder being taken in chains to the commandant's office. There the camp leader officially pardoned him, freed him of his chains, and allowed him to resume his ordinary camp life.

One day the inmates of our cage unloaded a ship that had arrived with a cargo of beds. The wives of the Djakarta residents had heard that their husbands had to sleep on the bare ground in the open or on the cement floor in the existing sheds. They had sought and received permission from the local police to send beds to our island camp. The police officers who accepted several dozen beds in this way and shipped them to Onrust evidently did not realize all the implications involved. They did not ask themselves whether it would be fair to provide beds for a minority of prisoners, while the majority, who came from locations farther removed than Djakarta, would not receive any. Furthermore, the sheds were hardly large enough to allow all inmates to sleep next to each other and would by no means have provided enough space for beds.

Anyway, I was one of the work detail ordered to unload the beds from the ship and pile them up in an open field next to the little harbor—in fact, in the same field we had left our suitcases the night of our arrival. Suddenly a man called out, "Siegfried Horn, here is your bed!" I looked and saw my name clearly written in the familiar handwriting of my wife, Jeanne, on tags attached to an iron bed and a mattress. We knew that we would not get the beds and that it would not even be fair to let us have them while most of the hundreds of prisoners would continue to sleep on the ground. However, I felt good inside to have seen this token of my wife's love and concern. It was also an indication that she was still free. That knowledge meant a lot to me because of the uncertainty in which we lived during those early days. We still had not received any mail from our loved ones.

As we unloaded that ship, we noticed that its hold contained quite a bit of dry straw that must have been used on a previous voyage as packing material. Each of us grabbed a small bundle of straw after we had completed our work, planning to use it as a kind of pillow. At the order to line up for the return march to our enclosure, we all stepped up with a bundle of straw under our arms. Seeing this, the sergeant shouted, "Put down the straw!" We all did so without a word of complaint or protest, but some of us would have liked to have torn him to pieces.

That night our island got one of its heavy tropical rain showers. We thought of both our mattresses and the straw that would rot in the open. In fact, a few days later another work detail of internees marched to the harbor and threw all beds and mattresses into the sea. Our wives, however, never knew this, and were happy in the illusion that we now had beds to sleep in.

The food situation was abominable at Onrust from beginning to end. We all lived through this period only because it lasted no longer than two months and because most of us were in a healthy condition when we arrived. The breakfasts were usually comprised of a small amount of hot cereal and so-called sandwiches. The latter consisted of a couple of dry slices of bread with so little jam that the bread looked as if someone had made thin crosses on them with a red pencil. Sometimes sardines took the place of jam. However, the few sardines were spread so sparingly on the dry slices of bread that we jokingly said that the kitchen people probably had nailed the sardines to the ceiling and threw the slices of bread against them in the hope that by touching them they would take on some of their smell.

Once a week we got a banana, the only fruit we ever saw, in a land where banana trees grow almost as weeds. Usually we could fill our bellies with rice at lunchtime when the main meal was served, but little meat or vegetable matter accompanied the rice.

Remembering what happened to Professor Thierfelder when he had asked for soap and cigarettes for his men, none of us ever dared to complain, but we were convinced that someone enriched himself on our empty stomachs. This became even more obvious at the following camp when our daily food rations were much more plentiful. The groceries we received there were of a much better quality and variety than they had ever been at Onrust. We all wondered how long we would have survived if the conditions at Onrust had continued in Sumatra.

Not only was the food situation lamentable, but also the mail service. Since we could receive only mail that had passed through the hands of a censor, and a censorship organization had still to be created when the war broke out, we had no communication with our relatives for several weeks. The simple reason for this painful situation was the complete lack of available trained censors. It took the authorities some time to set up such an office and find suitable and trustworthy people to operate it. It was therefore a red-letter day when a guard called me to the barbed-wire fence to receive the first postcard from my wife. It gave me proof that she was still free and continued to work as a nurse in our mission's maternity clinic, which she had founded two years earlier. It was a pity that we could not keep the cards. We had to read them quickly in the presence of the distributing soldier and return them to him. The authorities were evidently afraid that the cards contained some secret information or messages that had escaped the eyes of the censor.

That the conditions under which we lived were nibbling at our morale is understandable. Some men seemed to suffer more than others. The older men were definitely more affected than the younger ones. Like many others, I also asked a lot of questions: "Why did God allow this to happen?" "Why did our churches have to become orphans while we, who could have assisted them through the difficulties which they had to pass, were doomed to useless inactivity?" "Will our church members stand firm in severe trials?" Personal questions born of self-pity also went through my mind: "Will I retain my health and sanity if the living conditions, under which we vegetate, do not improve?" "Will my faith see me through and remain strong if my incarceration lasts several months or perhaps years?" "Will I become as cynical, gloomy, cantankerous, and currish as some others already are?"

I remember one day I discovered myself walking without purpose from one side of our fence to the other, back and forth. Suddenly I realized that I did exactly what I once had seen a tiger doing in the Djakarta zoo. It paced back and forth in its cage, while all the other tigers were lying quietly and peacefully. The animal's behavior was so strange that I asked one of the keepers why this one tiger was so nervous and the others not. He told me that the strangely behaving one had been recently caught and hadn't yet become accustomed to its new life. "Come back, in a couple of months," the man said, "and you will find it just as quiet as the others. It will get used to its life of captivity." Thinking of this experience in the Djakarta zoo, I asked myself, "Will this also happen to me?" When I later became reconciled with my lot and settled down to a routine life as a prisoner, I found out that the zookeeper's prediction was applicable not only to wild animals.

Then came a day of unmitigated misery. I had reached the point where I thought that I could not take it much longer. In fact, I was afraid that I might join the ranks of those who had already shown clear signs of mental derangement. Not only the physical deprivations and primitive conditions, but the lack of any reading material, the close association with constantly cursing sailors, political fanatics, and Nazis, and the absence of space for privacy, and, except during the night, no time for quiet meditation—all had plummeted me into a depression that bordered on mental exhaustion.

Just when I reached this low point we received news that we would get back our luggage. We had long ago given up hope of ever seeing it again. In fact, we thought the Dutch had cast it into the sea, as had happened to the beds our wives had sent us. However, we suddenly found out that our suitcases had all been stored in one of the empty sheds on the island and had not even suffered from the rain. It was a glorious announcement indeed. Finally my group marched to the shed where we searched among the hundreds of pieces of luggage for our own suitcases. I located mine and was glad that the inspecting officer found the contents of my suitcase not objectionable. With great joy I took it to my cage. Now I again had a toothbrush, a pair of scissors and a razor, soap and towels, also a pen and paper, and one item that I had missed more than anything else—my Bible.

After I returned to my enclosure, I put my suitcase on the spot where I slept, opened it, and removed my little Dutch Bible. Since it was too dark to read in the windowless shed I stepped outside, threw myself on the ground, and opened my Bible at random to Psalm 146. There my eye fell on a marginal handwritten note that read:

"Amsterdam, March 10, 1930. Fulfilled within two hours."

It was in January 1930, that I arrived in the Netherlands, coming from Stanborough College, Watford, England, where I had attended school. I was under appointment to the Dutch East Indies, but the mission board told me to learn the Dutch language first and to earn my living during the language study by selling Dutch religious publications. When I reached the harbor of Flushing the immigration officer asked me the purpose of my visit. I told him truthfully that I wanted to study the Dutch language and earn my living by colporteuring. He replied that the Netherlands had recently issued a law that did not allow aliens to engage in gainful work, since the country suffered serious unemployment because of worldwide economic conditions. The Great Depression that had begun with the crash on Wall Street in the autumn of 1929 had already made itself felt. Therefore the officer gave me a tourist visa for a few weeks and told me that I would need a statement from my mission board that would guarantee financial support during the time of my stay in the Netherlands before I could obtain a residence visa.

I wrote at once to the office of the Central European Division in Berlin, which controlled both the Netherlands Conference and the Netherlands East Indies Union Mission, and asked for advice. In due time I received word from Berlin, suggesting that I obtain the required visa in Amsterdam where I had settled. Thus on the day when my visa expired I presented myself to the immigration office in Amsterdam where I did not find a sympathetic hearing. The officer told me in no uncertain words that I either present proof that I could live on money that would come from outside the country or leave the Netherlands. If I would not comply with the requirement and consequently force the authorities to deport me, he said, the chances of ever getting a permit to go to a Dutch colony later on would be extremely slim. However, he extended my visa for a few more weeks.

It looked serious. Once again I contacted Berlin and reported the situation. Although I waited and waited for a reply, none came. On the day that my visa expired I found that the Morning Watch text read: "The Lord watches over the sojourners" (Ps. 146:9, RSV). It greatly encouraged me. Was I not a sojourner, or an alien, as the Dutch Bible expresses it? Would the Lord watch over me today, when I needed His help to obtain the necessary permit to stay in the country, so that I could learn the language that I must know in my assigned mission field?

Feeling better, I went downtown, but the closer I came to the building housing the immigration office, the more I lost heart. Arriving in front of its monumental staircase I was afraid to enter. Instead, I walked around the block to build up my courage and delay the fateful confrontation with the stern official with whom I had talked a few weeks earlier. Twice more I went around the block, then decided I would have to face him anyway.

When I reached the desk where I had received a somewhat harsh reception some weeks earlier I noticed a different man sat at it. I placed before him my request for a residence visa. He asked me for what purpose I wanted it, and I replied that I was under appointment to the Dutch East Indies, but wanted first to learn the Dutch language. The officer asked no more questions, but stamped my passport, gave it to me, and wished me good luck. As soon as I left the office I checked to find out what kind of visa I had received. To my delight, I discovered that it was a permanent residence visa. Going home, I thanked God for having heard my prayers and allowing me such a marvelous experience of seeing a biblical promise answered so quickly. It was then that I wrote on the margin the already mentioned text: "Amsterdam, March 10, 1930. Fulfilled within two hours."

As I saw the note, the experience instantly flashed through my mind. Let me read this psalm and see whether it also contains a message for me that applies to my present situation, I thought to myself. So I began to scan Psalm 146, beginning with verse 1. At verse 7 I noticed the words: "The Lord sets the prisoners free" (RSV).

It was exactly the promise I needed in my utterly depressed state. In fact, I expected the Lord to fulfill it just as promptly as He had done 10 years earlier. I therefore expected an officer to appear that afternoon at our fence with the message to me that I could pack my things and go home. But I waited in vain that day and the next and many more to come. Not until the autumn of 1946, more than six years after I read the promise, could I write on the margin of Psalm 146:7 that it was finally fulfilled in Bombay.

However, let me say this: I did experience the literal fulfillment of both promises, one within two hours after I had read it, the other after nearly 2,300 days—the longest prophetic period in the Bible (Dan. 8:14). Fulfilled they were, but as it became clear to me much later, each in its own divinely appointed time so that God's purpose for my life work could be carried out. It was something that I neither knew or understood when my internment started.

Anyway, this experience on the little island of Onrust, while not changing the physical conditions of my incarceration, resulted in an immediate change in my outlook on life. My depression disappeared. Able to smile again, I stopped my obsession with my own misery. Now I tried to pierce the dark future and started to lay plans about what I would do when freedom would come. Also I began for the first time to reckon with the possibility that my imprisonment, so unjust and senseless as it seemed to be, might possibly have a hidden blessing, that I might have to fulfill a divine purpose unknown to me at that time. It was then that I asked myself, "What can I do with my time, the only thing left to me?"

It was wonderful to have access to a Bible once more. My having the Bible dictionary suggested that I should do some kind of Bible study in which it could be useful. The idea occurred to me that I should see what I could learn about little known individuals of the Bible. I began to work on the many names of men listed or mentioned in the books of Ezra and Nehemiah to see what I could discover about them. Soon I found the study much more interesting and even more exciting than I had expected.

With my mind engaged in doing something, the days passed much more quickly than before. My studies might not have seemed visibly profitable, but I learned things I had not known before. As long as the hours of daylight permitted me to read, I kept at it. That the studies involved some physical discomforts the reader will understand, when he realizes that at Onrust we had neither tables nor chairs. We had to do everything—eating, sleeping, or studying—by sitting or lying on the ground in the open or, when it rained, on the cement floor in a semidark shed. Nevertheless I found myself saying one day that I regretted that the days were so short and that I wished we had some light in the evenings so that they would not be wasted.

In the meantime news reached us through the grapevine that the Dutch authorities were building a camp in Sumatra for us and that they would soon transport us there. Convinced that no camp could be worse than the one that we occupied, I looked forward to the move, since it would also bring a welcome change in the monotony of our primitive existence. Therefore I was glad when I found myself part of the first group of several hundred men to leave Onrust for an unknown destination. Later we learned that the new camp was still under construction and could not absorb at once all those on the island of Onrust.

After a two-month stay at Onrust each of those who belonged to the first transport received a uniform consisting of green shorts and a shirt, a straw hat like those worn by the soldiers, underwear, socks, and a pair of shoes. Thus neatly dressed we traveled in a naval minesweeper back to Tanjung Priok, the harbor of Djakarta. There newspaper photographers had already assembled to take pictures of us as we transferred to a combination freighter and passenger ship of the Royal Packet Navigation Company (KPM), which made regular runs from Djakarta to Medan in North Sumatra via Singapore. The next day pictures appeared in the newspapers showing us all neatly dressed in brand-new uniforms and appearing fit and well.

In fact, many of the internees looked better than before their arrest, since the loss of weight—in some cases as much as 50 pounds—had not hurt their appearance for they had been grossly overweight to begin with. Only in Sumatra did the prolonged undernourishment reveal its detrimental effect on our physical condition by lowering our resistance to infection. However, the newspaper pictures, gave the impression that our internment was a humane affair, and if we were even given new clothing for our transfer from Java to Sumatra we had nothing to complain about. How easily appearances can be deceptive!

While heavily armed soldiers guarded us on this trip and we rode in the hold of the ship we were treated quite decently on the three-day voyage to Medan. We made the trip from that harbor city to our new camp at Kotatjane in Atjeh, the northernmost province of Sumatra, in moving vans, as well as in open and closed trucks. I was fortunate to be in an open truck. Although surrounded by a contraption of wooden beams and barbed wire, we could watch the scenery of the lush tropical mountain countryside through which we traveled. Since it was all new to me I enjoyed the day-long trip through the jungles and plantations.

Those in moving vans or fully closed trucks were not so fortunate. Transported in semidarkness, they could not see anything of the outside world, and, because of poor ventilation, had to spend the whole day in frightfully foul and hot air. Some even thought they would never live to see the new camp. One van had the misfortune of slipping on one of the many hairpin curves of the mountain roads and tumbling into a ravine that was luckily not too deep. Although one of the accompanying soldiers riding in the cab was thrown out and crushed by the heavy vehicle, all the internees survived. However, several had broken bones and other injuries.

Chapter III

In the Jungles of Sumatra

Our trip continued well after dark, and we were all eager for the dusty and bumpy ride on unpaved roads to come to an end. We also wanted to find out what the new camp was like and how it would compare with Onrust. Finally we reached a lovely valley—the Alas Valley—and entered a large clearing in the dense jungle. The first thing we noticed, with satisfaction, was that the site had electric lights, dispelling the fear that, just as at Onrust, we would be forced to waste the evening hours in the dark.

Our caravan of trucks and vans stopped in front of a sizable wooden gate to a large, barbed-wire enclosed compound, the first of six such compounds to be completed. It would receive the designation Block A, or Wing A. After the guards unloaded and admitted us to this wing, I went out at once on an inspection tour. After two months in a camp with cramped cages, hardly any space to move, and under the most primitive conditions imaginable, our first impression was favorable as far as we could tell in the dark, with electric lights shining only over selected areas and inside the various barracks.

We saw that the wing contained 10 wooden sleeping barracks, four dining halls, one barracks designated to serve as a hospital, one to be the canteen, and another one to be the kitchen. There were also wooden toilet and shower facilities built over an open water channel, which we guessed came from a mountain stream. The channel ran through our wing from one end to the other. A barbed-wire fence surrounded the whole wing instead of around every single barracks as at Onrust. The guards watched from wooden towers at the four corners of our wing, but outside of the fence. I felt that we 500 inmates could live here more decently as a community than at Onrust. Now we had some space to walk, could enjoy a measure of privacy, and could take care of our own food preparation. Also our own interned doctors would provide medical care.

My missionary friend Andy Krautschick and I, who had shared joys and sorrows from the second day of our internment, selected one of the sleeping barracks. We found it to be a long windowless wooden structure with a thatched roof. It had a door at each end with a long walkway through the center. On both sides of the walkway wooden boards nailed to horses stretched from one end of the barracks to the other end. On the boards lay empty straw sacks, one lying next to the other. The guards told us that straw would be made available later on. However, Andy, I, and many other men never stuffed the sacks with straw and used it only to fill our pillowcases. Our wooden boards with empty sacks lying on them felt like foam rubber mattresses after having slept for more than two months on the bare cement floor.

After a comparatively good meal on our first night at the new camp we bedded down, reasonably satisfied with our housing arrangements. When a bell roused us the next morning to assemble for the first roll call—which now took place twice daily—the first thing we saw were monkeys jumping from tree to tree in the dense jungle that surrounded our camp. It seemed to us that they looked at us with utter amazement and glee, marveling that the wildest monkey dream had come true. Now at last people were put into cages as in a zoo while monkeys were free to come and go and to gawk at them to their hearts' desire.

After the first roll call our new camp commandant addressed us. He had been the director of a civil prison. We learned that from now on we would be under the control of a civil administration, and that only professional jailers and wardens would enter our compounds. The military would be responsible merely to guard us and make sure that none of us would escape. Also he informed us of the camp rules, which the authorities later issued in written form and occasionally supplemented by additional regulations. Some of the rules were much more sensible than the ones under which we had lived at Onrust. The penalties for violations were much more humane and no longer garnished with numerous threats of execution.

Within days we settled down to a more or less normal life. We even began to alter our barracks. While the administration of our camp did not encourage the changes, they did not oppose them either. The principal need of our builders, craftsmen, and artisans were tools. They made them from long iron nails and other structural iron parts of our barracks that our architects considered superfluous in the existing structures. In this way most of us obtained knives made of long flattened nails. We also produced garden implements, saws, and other cutting, grinding, polishing, and engraving tools in the same manner. The first thing we did after fashioning tools was to dismantle our sleeping structures and create bunk beds. By doing this we generated more space. We constructed a narrow bench and a tiny table for each two people so they had space to sit as well as room to walk between their beds. Furthermore, we cut small windows into the walls between the beds to provide some light for our barracks to make their interiors more cheerful.

Not only did we thus improve our living spaces, but quite a few men possessing all kinds of other skills began to apply them. Some men planted small gardens between the barracks and raised vegetables and fast-growing plants and fruit trees, such as green peppers and papayas, to supplement our meager diet. Others made themselves useful by constructing raised footpaths and digging trenches to drain the rainwater away from our barracks so that we could get from the sleeping barracks to the dining halls or the bathrooms without walking ankle-deep in mud.

Two or three instrument makers even made violins, cellos, and other musical instruments. In this way the musicians in our camp, of whom we had a considerable number, started an orchestra. First they entertained us by performing on glass bottles tuned to a particular pitch of the scale by filling them with water to various levels. Later they replaced the bottles with all kinds of musical instruments fashioned in camp. Eventually the camp allowed them to purchase instruments from the outside market. The internees also produced many chessboards and artistically carved chess figures.

Our professional cooks took over the kitchen and produced culinary miracles with the items they received as our daily ration. They did so without the use of refrigerators or appliances of any kind, and doing all cooking for hundreds of internees on woodburning open fireplaces.

Another lively activity that began soon after our arrival was the organization of all types of classes. Although we badly felt the lack of books, blackboards, paper, and ink in the beginning, many young people were eager to use the opportunity that our enforced period of inactivity provided, to profit from the knowledge and skills of the large number of professionals in the camp. Language classes were especially popular. A number requested me to start a class in English, which I later exchanged for teaching Hebrew and New Testament Greek when I obtained books. We also asked the professionals to provide lectures on topics ranging from volcanology, tropical medicine, history, and physical anthropology, to winemaking, beer brewing, or political science. Some lectures—for example, the latter—were more popular than others.

It does not mean that our wing had the appearance of a human ant hill. Not all the men were industrious or eager to work or make themselves useful. The lazy men suffered more from being deprived of their freedom than those who kept themselves busy. Some men were passionate chess or card players and never seemed to tire of those activities. Others lay all day long on their beds thinking of their families and worrying about them, with the result that in the end they suffered mental exhaustion or derangement. We had several pitiable cases of men among us who took their lives because they could no longer cope with being imprisoned. More than one man I knew hanged himself.

I remember one man who took a long nail and pounded it with a stone into his forehead. The nail entered between the two brain lobes and did not destroy any vital brain cells. When his friends discovered him lying in his blood on his bed, they took him to the doctor, who pulled out the nail. He quickly recovered from his wound. Still determined to take his life, in another attack of insanity he climbed to the top of the water tower while everyone was eating at lunch, and jumped. Although he broke both legs, he did not die. The camp administration then had him removed to an insane asylum. I do not know what happened to him after that.

One man who lived in my barracks for several months had no interests whatsoever and could talk of nothing but his wonderful wife and lovely children. While we sympathized with him, we soon tired of his self-pity. Hardly anybody wanted to talk with him, so he spent most of his time lying on his bed longing for freedom. Then came a postcard from his wife asking him for a divorce, as she had fallen in love with another man. Crushed, the poor man refused to eat. A few days later some of us carried him on a stretcher to the camp hospital, where he died within a short time of a broken heart.

The confined life of scores of men in each barrack also revealed an individual's true character. Actions and habits quickly betrayed to the other inmates whether he was a saint or sinner. We made the acquaintance of wonderful men—some of them professing no religion—who were always cheerful, helpful, ready to do small favors or go a second mile. They were selfless, kind, and the friend of everyone. One of them became my lifelong friend.

But then there were also the sour and sullen ones, who, often angry over nothing, could get excited or irritated by trivial inconveniences or offenses. Since all tried to avoid them, they were lonely, sad men. The bunk bed of my close friend Andy and me bordered on that of such a man. Occasionally it happened that one of our suitcases, which we stored on the floor beneath our bed, unintentionally got pushed into his living space by one or two inches. He could erupt into uncontrolled rage, since he always interpreted such incidents as premeditated, malicious, and willful attempts to arouse his anger. Most of us took the customary Javanese nap after lunch. When this unhappy man could not sleep, he became upset and woke up everyone in his vicinity by his loud complaints about the injustice of being doomed to remain awake and listen to everyone else snore.

This was the life to which we all had to adjust. It was one of routine. Twice a day we had to stand in line for roll calls, three times we met for the daily meals in the dining barracks, once a week we helped for half a day in the kitchen peeling potatoes, cutting onions, and washing and preparing vegetables. For the remainder of the time we were free to do what we wanted.

Twice a week we received mail in the form of postcards, which usually showed the work of the censor through material blacked out with India ink. We had to read the cards in the presence of the wardens and then return them. And twice a week each one of us could mail one postcard to our correspondents.

It was a happy day when we learned, about six months after our internment started, that the government had decided to allow us to receive newspapers. The announcement ended our long and painfully felt isolation from the outside world. Papers had occasionally made their way into our camp, but since this was illegal and dangerous, it was most unsatisfactory. Once the authorities discovered a newspaper in the bottom of a sack of rice. They led the Chinese merchant who furnished the rice away in handcuffs and leg chains. A Dutch officer later told our cooks that the man would probably be executed for having had illicit contact with the enemy in time of war. Whether it really happened we never found out. But somehow the underground channels through which newspapers occasionally reached us were never completely cut off.

It was always a cause of great joy when news reports penetrated our camp. Naval officers trained to transmit messages by arm and hand signals between ships now passed them along from one wing to another. They placed themselves inside a barracks close to the fence with the door open, so that another such officer in the adjoining wing could see them. Such clandestine activities ended when we were officially allowed to receive newspapers. Every afternoon men gathered for a half hour around someone fluent in translating the most important parts of the paper from Dutch into German, since many internees could not read or understand Dutch. Many of them looked forward to this daily half hour newspaper reading with keen anticipation.

Not long after newspapers began to enter our camp legally, I came across one issue that contained an item about my wife. Since she had been born of Dutch parents in Holland, the government had not restricted her movements, as it had those of the German women. Many of them were interned or restricted to their homes until they had an opportunity to leave the country. While Jeanne was thus free to come and go and continue her work as a nurse in the mission's maternity clinic in Djakarta, she nevertheless had to report daily to the local police station. Once when she was ill and bedridden for several days, she had to force herself to report on the first day of her illness, although the police from then on sent an officer to her home every day to check on her until she was well.

But now, about seven or eight months after the outbreak of the war, the government, in response to her petition, had officially declared her to be a "nonenemy alien." It freed her both from reporting to the police and from obtaining a written permit to travel whenever she wanted to leave Djakarta in order to visit friends in Bandung, Bogor, or elsewhere. I was naturally happy when I read the official decision that she was no longer considered an enemy alien and would be spared any further harassment.

A rather unpleasant chapter of our internment was the constant battle with diseases and sicknesses. At Onrust we had no mosquito nets, thus exposing us to the tropical scourge of malaria. It was only weeks later that we received quinine pills to fight the dreadful disease. Many prisoners succumbed to it and had attacks at regular intervals. In fact, for several weeks the only medicine that entered our camp on the island of Onrust was castor oil, which was handed out for all and every ailment. Even in the new camp at Alas Valley, medical service was nonexistent in the beginning. The fact that we had among us many excellent physicians and medical specialists was hardly of any benefit to us as long as they had neither instruments nor medicines.

One case, in which I played a small role, remained indelibly imprinted on my mind. A Lutheran missionary among my acquaintances became violently ill. The doctors' diagnosis was acute appendicitis. They told the patient that he would lose his life if the badly inflamed appendix were not removed. He was also informed that removing his appendix would involve surgery without anesthesia under the primitive conditions under which we lived. He urged our doctors to operate to save his life.

The surgeon borrowed a sharp knife from the kitchen and also some sewing needles and strong thread from a man who had brought a sewing kit into the camp, and tried to make them thoroughly sterile by boiling them in water. First he had the patient's abdomen well scrubbed. After that, the missionary was placed faceup on a table, while several of us strong young men, as instructed, held him down firmly so that he could not move at all. While the operation lasted only about 15 or 20 minutes, it was an eternity for the patient, who suffered excruciating pain. During the incision he screamed with a penetrating, shrill voice. However, he went into shock quickly and lost consciousness, so that he just whimpered during much of the procedure. The operation was successful, and the man recovered nicely.

Another patient was not so lucky. He also needed an abdominal operation to save his life. The physician performed the surgery in a similar manner. Unfortunately, a bird flew into the barracks during the operation. It landed on a horizontal beam of the thatched roof above the patient, and just at that time lost some of its droppings, which fell exactly into the patient's open abdomen. Although the surgeons removed as much of the waste as they could, they feared the worst. Having no medications to fight any infection or blood poisoning, they gave the patient little hope to survive the ordeal. He died a few days later.

I myself had my share of sicknesses during the 17 months of my enforced sojourn in Sumatra. The first began a few days after our arrival. Reaching the new camp, we were happy to see that we had water. We never had enough water in Onrust, since the authorities had to ship every drop from mainland Java to our camp. To our great joy Alas Valley had a stream running through the camp. Now we could take showers as often as we wanted, and had plenty of water for washing our clothes, for meeting the kitchen's needs, and also for draining our wastes away.

What we did not know was that our running water came from a mountain stream that had already passed through two villages where it served as toilets as such streams do everywhere in the interior of Sumatra. While the kitchen personnel boiled the water before dispensing it to us, no one warned us to refrain from rinsing our dishes and spoons in it after our meals.

The result was that within days of our arrival a vicious bacillary dysentery epidemic broke out in our wing. First a few men fell ill, then one or two days later a large number of men came down with this disease. When several men died, not only our doctors became alarmed, but also the camp administration. After all, no one in authority favored a mass extinction of the camp inmates. The administration issued rules to isolate all sick people from those not yet affected, and described how to treat the water before using it. The Dutch authorities converted several of the dining halls into sick bays and ordered medicine from Java, which they had flown to

Medan, the city closest to our camp. They brought hundreds of pots de chambre from the nearest city and made them available. Crates of oranges and other food that would restore health after a bout with the dreaded disease—items which we had not seen for more than two months—began to arrive. In this way the administration stemmed the spread of the epidemic in a comparatively short time and reduced the number of fatalities.

I joined the ranks of the patients on the third or fourth day after the outbreak of the dysentery epidemic. Within a day or two I was so sick that I lost the courage to fight the disease and told my friends that I no longer cared whether I lived or not. The intestinal cramps had become practically unbearable. Our doctors tried to save as many lives as possible. Among them was Dr. Mengert, a physician whom I had known for years, since he had been the house doctor of several of my church members and had also treated my wife.

On the evening of the third day of my illness Mengert came to me and tried to encourage me not to lose my will to live. "Horn, I believe that tonight will be the turning point for you," he said. "I will stay at your bed throughout the night to help you. If you make it till morning, there is hope for you." I know little of that night since I spent it in a half delirium, but when day broke the doctor told me that he had given me several injections during the night, forced me repeatedly to drink orange juice and some weak tea, and was convinced that I would recuperate.

He was right. Although it took several weeks to recover, I was completely healed from that dreadful disease, except that the violent bowel movements had torn my bowels in one spot, which produced a bleeding wound that eventually became a cyst. Later I had it surgically removed in India, where we had good medical facilities in our fifth and last internment camp.

Another problem we faced in the first and second camps was the lack of dental care. Our internees included good dentists, but they could do nothing but extract teeth with pairs of pliers, the only dental instruments available to them. Because of our undernourishment and perhaps also as a result of my illness, several of my teeth began to give me trouble. When my toothaches increased I consulted Dr. Ziegler, a well-known dentist who had practiced in Bandung before the war. He examined my teeth and told me that four molars had cavities and needed attention badly. Since he could do nothing to them in camp except extract them, he advised me to have them removed. Pointing out how tragic it would be to lose four good teeth at the age of 33, I protested. "To lose four teeth is better than to lose an arm or leg in the war, as so many of our citizens at home are obliged to give up," he replied.

So I consented to have the troublemakers removed, not expecting that it would result in more pain than I had ever experienced before. One tooth broke off and the roots remained in my jaw with a raw, exposed nerve. Dr. Ziegler told me that I would have to wait until the roots worked themselves out so that he could extract them, since he had no special instrument to deal with them until then. In a similar case he had broken a jawbone. Not having any painkilling medicines either, he predicted that I would suffer quite a bit of discomfort and pain until the nerve would die by itself.

His prophecy was fulfilled to the very letter. Suffering indescribable pain, I could hardly eat, since every movement of my jaw produced agony. I slept little at night and could not find the energy or concentration of mind to read or study during the day. Never before or after did I ever go through such a miserable time. The pain subsided after several days as the nerve slowly died and eventually disappeared completely. After several months I could feel with my tongue that the roots had worked themselves out of the gum. When I reported this to the dentist he extracted them with a pair of pliers without any trouble.

Chapter IV

A Prisoner's Life of Study

I have already mentioned the role classes played in camp life. In this chapter I want to describe my own program of study and teaching, which I carried out all through the years of my internment. Since my activities in the Sumatra camp and three subsequent camps were interrupted only for short periods of time when we were moved from one camp to another, and were not materially altered in scope or nature, I will telescope them into one account.

One of the most welcome announcements in our second camp occurred shortly after our arrival in Sumatra. It informed us that we could receive books from our own libraries as long as they were not of a political nature. Naturally only those of us whose wives were not in an internment camp could take advantage of it, principally those whose wives were either Dutch or native-born women.

As soon as I heard it I wrote out an application to the camp commandant to allow my wife to ship to me the books named in an attached list. It contained about 70 volumes, such as my copies of the Bible in Hebrew and Greek, grammars and dictionaries of biblical Hebrew and Greek, a three-volume history of Israel, and a volume on the life of Christ in French. Quite a few of the books dealt with biblical archaeology—my special hobby. Among them was a volume on Hebrew letters of the sixth century B.C., discovered a few years previously at biblical Lachish in Palestine, and a volume on the Canaanite literary documents found during the excavations at Ugarit on the north Syrian coast. I intended to use them to refresh my knowledge of Hebrew, Greek, and French, and keep me busy in case our internment should last for several months or even a year or two. A longer incarceration I did not dare to think about, for such a thought seemed to me almost sinful, since it could be interpreted as an expression of doubt in God's ability to return our freedom to us.

On the other hand, I considered the unexpected permission to obtain books from my own library as an opportunity to improve my time. How many occasions in years past had I said to myself and others that I wished I had time for research. My busy life as a missionary during the Depression years, when every one of us had to do the work of two or three men, had left me little opportunity for real study. I even had feared that my knowledge of biblical Hebrew, which I had learned in a private Jewish school as a child, was slipping way from me. Also my French and New Testament Greek from college was disappearing. Now I had all the time that for years I had longed to have. It was up to me to make the most of it.

When I showed my application and list to one of my friends before I sent them to the camp commandant, he said to me, "Siegfried, you are crazy! Use your brain! This long list will land in the wastepaper basket. Ask for two or three books and after receiving them, send for some more. In this way you can gradually build up a library." I thanked him for his advice, but did not follow it. Instead I sent off my application as written. Later I learned that the commandant approved it and that Jeanne received it in due time.

She then picked the desired volumes from my book shelves and packed them in two wooden boxes to ship to our camp. By taxi she went to the police headquarters in Djakarta and requested the officer in charge to forward the boxes to me. When he saw them and learned that the 70 books were for one internee, he exploded. "What do you think we are here for, Mrs. Horn? We would have to read all these books! If you had brought one book or two we might do it, but not a whole library. There is no way of getting us to do that."

So she turned around and had herself driven to the local military headquarters. There she discovered that they had nothing to do with prisoner camps of civilian internees and therefore could not help her.

Jeanne, always the resourceful person, did not give up. She remembered that I had been well acquainted with the chief of the Dutch secret police. The man had needed my help in dealing with Chinese Adventist colporteurs. Although they carried letters of recommendation from the office of the Seventh-day Adventist China Division in Shanghai, the Dutch authorities did not trust such papers, since they were afraid that Communists might be slipping into the country under the guise of being Christian salesmen. They had learned by experience that letters of recommendation, even from Christian organizations, could be faked, and offered no guarantee that the carrier was a trustworthy, nonpolitical salesman of Chinese Christian literature.

When such a man landed in Djakarta, the chief of the secret police would phone me. "Mr. Horn, we have here a man from your outfit in Shanghai. Would you look him over and give us your opinion about him." In such a case I would drive to the harbor of Tanjung Priok armed with the *Seventh-day Adventist Yearbook*. With an interpreter provided by the secret police, I would then interrogate him. I would ask him about the names of certain officers of the division whom he should know if he was a genuine Adventist colporteur, and question him about Adventist teachings and the contents of the books he wanted to sell. In most cases I could recommend that the men be admitted to the country. I evidently made no mistakes, because I never heard of any complaints. In one or two cases I was not sure of the man's claims, and reported so. The colonial authorities then sent him back to China. In time I requested the China Division to alert me about the arrival of anyone whom they sent to the East Indies with their recommendation, so that I would know what to do. This worked quite well and as a result the chief of the secret police and I developed a good relationship during my years in Djakarta.

Remembering this, my wife asked the taxi driver to take her to his office in Tanjung Priok, the harbor of Djakarta. She told him that the commandant of her husband's camp in Sumatra had approved his request to receive the 70 study books she had packed but no agency was willing to ship them to me. He explained that, although he had nothing to do with the affairs of the German internees, he knew enough people in authority to get the two boxes of books delivered, saying, "Mr. Horn helped us many times during the past few years. I will do this for him."

Soon thereafter I received word from the camp commandant's office to come with a few of my friends to pick up the boxes of books. There was great surprise throughout our camp when the news spread that I had received such a large number of books, which for the duration of our internment formed the largest private library any internee possessed. In fact, the camp authorities withdrew the permit to obtain books from our own libraries even before those ordered under the initial announcement had arrived. The censors quickly realized that they could not handle the influx of so many parcels.

Nevertheless, those of us interested in serious study were happy that several hundred volumes had entered the camp and we made a union catalog of all available titles and loaned them to each other. Since I was the only prisoner who owned both Greek and Hebrew grammars, the two books were in constant demand for copying by those who had enrolled in my Greek and Hebrew classes. Such heavy use wore them out and we had to rebind them in camp to prevent the leaves from getting lost. My Hebrew grammar was therefore rebound once by means of primitive tools and the use of some cloth from a pair of discarded pants, while my Greek grammar was rebound twice in this manner. I myself copied by hand a whole Latin grammar before I joined a Latin class.

At that time I switched from teaching English, which I had done so far without the help of any books, to Greek and Hebrew. When it became known that I was proficient in biblical languages, several missionaries, both Protestant and Catholic, requested that I form classes so they could learn those languages they had failed to study during their seminary training. I taught with interruptions for several years.

The teaching experience aided me when I arrived in America after the war. In my youth I had attended the Friedensau Mission Seminary in Germany, as well as Stanborough College in England, but had earned no degree since both institutions were neither senior colleges nor accredited. In order to earn a bachelor's degree I enrolled at Walla Walla College as soon as I came to the United States in the fall of 1946. It was the time when many ex-GIs went back to college, and there were so many young men enrolled in Greek classes at Walla Walla College that the school did not have enough teachers available. When the administration learned that I had taught Greek during the war years, it asked me to conduct two

Greek classes at the same time I worked toward my degree. As a result I earned enough money to see me through my studies until I had my degree.

My prison studies began in earnest when I acquired the books. First I spent quite a bit of time working through the Greek and Hebrew grammars to become fully proficient in the two biblical languages. Done with that I decided to translate the whole Bible from the original languages into German. I wanted to become fully acquainted with its contents as well as with the problems a translator faces. I felt that one could not reach both goals by translating only selected passages or easy-to-read books such as the historical ones.

Consequently I decided to devote a fixed number of hours to it every day, working on both the Hebrew Old Testament and the Greek New Testament, and to write out my translation in longhand. I began the project at the Sumatra camp in the fall of 1940, completing the translation of the New Testament in March 1943, and that of the Old Testament a year later, in March 1944. Next I decided to read daily two pages in my Hebrew Bible and two pages in the Greek New Testament, an exercise I have continued with some interruptions, to the present time.

Also I continued to study deeply into the postexilic history of the Jews as far as the end of the Old Testament. I found the subject matter so exciting and fascinating that I used every free minute not needed for classwork, translation of the Bible, or other routine activities.

In fact, I became so fanatical in the use of my time that I rose earlier in the morning than usual if, on a preceding day, I had lost some time in my study schedule through unexpected interruptions such as inspections by the camp commandant. Also, on days when I did my weekly laundry I got up an hour earlier. You can easily understand that some of my friends considered such behavior ridiculous or even slightly abnormal. I remember how one of them assured me that if I kept it up I would soon be hoping that we would not be freed until I had completed all my projects.

Anyway, in 1944 I assembled all my notes and wrote a history of Judah from Zerubbabel to Nehemiah, a manuscript of 347 handwritten pages. Although I have never published it or any of my other camp-produced manuscripts, it proved of great value when about 10 years later I wrote the commentary to the books Ezra and Nehemiah for the *Seventh-day Adventist Bible Commentary,* volume 3.

Another project on which I worked for some time was the matter of Old Testament chronology. The subject had interested me for many years, since without exception all biblical historians claimed that the problems of biblical chronology were insoluble. In the course of years I had acquired many, if not nearly all, the published studies in the field and had learned which scholars used which methods to deal with the manifold problems of the calendrical and chronological systems employed by the ancient Hebrews. I had learned what accession years and nonaccession years were, what predating or postdating means, which nations followed civil or religious or both types of calendars, what the difference was between a regnal and a calendar year, who used a solar or lunar or even a luni-solar calendar, or what an embolismic year and an intercalary month was. With this preliminary knowledge I set to work and by trial and error attempted to find solutions to the numerous problems of Old Testament chronology.

My research never led me to a full harmony of all biblical data. But I came to the point where I saw that I could not expect to make any further progress in my work. Therefore I decided to write up the results I had reached so far, thus producing a handwritten manuscript of 158 pages.

When I came to America in 1946 I learned that E. R. Thiele, an Adventist professor at Emmanuel Missionary College (Andrews University), had apparently solved all the problems of the chronology of the Hebrew kings. At once I contacted him and obtained his published article. To my great surprise and real joy I found that our systems were identical in many parts, but that he had found a plausible explanation for several problem texts on the reigns of the last kings of Israel. When I received this help I found that with one exception, the other problem texts, which even Thiele had not satisfactorily explained, now fell into place. Several years later an Australian Adventist missionary-scholar explained even that text to my satisfaction.

The author of "Chronology" in volume 2 of *The Seventh-Day Adventist Bible Commentary* later took over this system of biblical chronology worked out by the combined efforts of an American scholar, a former German prisoner and an Australian missionary. Again the time spent behind barbed wire proved to have been useful and beneficial for something.

For a long time I had been aware of my lack of knowledge of the New Testament. Whether it was because of my deep interest in biblical archaeology, which illuminates the Old Testament more than the New, or to a special, perhaps innate, love for the Old Testament, I cannot say. Several years before my imprisonment I had decided to do something about my deficiency and had actually purchased four New Testament commentary sets, several volumes on introductory matters, and various books on the history of the New Testament canon and times. A lack of time had prevented me, however, from making more than a meager beginning.

When I made out the list of books I wanted from my library, I included a good number on the New Testament. However, I had already made plans to work on biblical chronology and on the history of postexilic Israel, as well as to translate the whole Bible. Therefore, I put any intensive study of the New Testament on the back burner, and it remained there for several years.

Only after I completed my three major projects did I devote the major part of my available time for an entire year to the study of the New Testament. At the end of that year I had produced a handwritten manuscript of 546 pages that covered the language and text of the New Testament, the early Christian literature, the history of the canon and of New Testament times, the life and message of Jesus, and the apostolic and postapostolic ages.

While I never again specialized in New Testament studies, that year made my later ministry and teaching more meaningful. It also prevented me from becoming too one-sided in outlook and emphasis.

So far I have not mentioned my greatest interest—biblical archaeology, a subject by no means neglected or crowded out by the other projects on which I constantly worked. No, I believe that hardly a day went by during the many years of my imprisonment that I did not read something on archaeological subjects and make prolific notes. Soon I had many handwritten pages on the topic.

First I used the material to work out several series of archaeological lectures to which I subjected my three close Adventist missionary friends who shared the same wing with me in one of our camps in India. We had formed a small colloquium and presented the fruits of our individual studies to each other in weekly get-togethers.

After that I decided to produce manuscripts on two archaeology-related subjects, first "An Archaeological Commentary to the Old Testament," and second a "History of Biblical Archaeological Exploration in the Bible Lands." By the time my imprisonment ended, I had completed a total of 660 manuscript pages on the two projects. Although I never completed them, I had the two manuscripts bound in later years to serve as memorials of the last two great projects on which I worked as a prisoner.

The work on the two projects that I planned to make the masterpieces of my literary prison activities was certainly not spent in vain. In fact, it bore much fruit in the future. First, it enabled me to teach a college course on biblical archaeology at Walla Walla College during the first year after my release from prison camp. Second, it gave direction to my graduate study program after having earned a bachelor's degree. And third, it secured for me the position of professor of archaeology and history of antiquity at the Seventh-day Adventist Theological Seminary, where I taught for 26 years.

Chapter V

Saved From Death by Mistake

By the middle of 1941 our prison life had become somewhat routine. One day followed another in a monotonous sameness. Occasionally the newspapers we regularly received brought excitement into our camp. We followed with great interest the conquests of Yugoslavia and Greece, the capture of Crete by parachutists, the seesaw battles in northern Africa, and the unending fight of the Allies against the German submarines that formed an increasing menace to their international shipping lanes.

However, the war hardly affected us personally and we therefore followed its events more with interest than involvement. Then the situation changed suddenly. In June 1941 the news that Germany had started to invade the Soviet Union hit the camp like a bombshell. Some of us wondered whether Hitler's invasion of Russia would end in utter defeat, as Napoleon's disastrous invasion had more than 100 years earlier. How could a small (though powerful) nation like Germany overcome a giant, three times Germany's size in population and 30 times in area? Was it not a suicidal, insane undertaking? Although many of us asked such questions, no one dared to voice them publicly since the Nazi members among our camp population had already threatened everyone to expect severe punishment after the war if they showed any signs of defeatism or anti-Nazism.

Yet the entry of the Soviet Union into war affected a large portion of our internees directly and caused them anxiety and fear for their loved ones' safety. The wives and children of a number of our prisoners were, according to the previously announced travel schedule, on the Trans-Siberian Railroad somewhere between Vladivostok and Germany.

After the German invasion of the Netherlands, practically all male Germans living in the Dutch East Indies were interned, and most of their families were put into separate camps. Only the Dutch-born wives, such as Jeanne, and those born in the East Indies escaped imprisonment. Soon the Germans, through a neutral government, began to seek the release of the German wives and their children in the Netherlands East Indies. After several months of slow negotiations between the governments of Germany, Russia, and Japan (the latter two had not yet entered the war) and the government of the Netherlands East Indies, they reached an agreement that would allow the German families—without their husbands and sons above the age of 16 years—to travel to Japan and from there through Russia to Germany.

Consequently, the Japanese dispatched two passenger liners to Java. Just a few weeks before Germany's invasion of Russia the first of them picked up many German families to take them to Vladivostok. As far as our men knew, they had already left Vladivostok for Germany when Hitler's attack occurred.

It is not hard to understand the terrible worry under which the internees lived and suffered. What would the Russians do to the innocent families? Would they be put into concentration camps in the murderous climate of Siberia? How would they be treated? Would we ever see them again? These and many similar questions plagued those who knew that their families had already departed. The agony under which these men lived and suffered was indescribable. Many could not eat. Some acted as if they were on the verge of losing their mind, while others talked of suicide. Those of us not directly affected by this new situation naturally lived in full sympathy with our suffering friends.

The Swiss consul, who represented the German affairs in the Netherlands East Indies, received a barrage of telegrams urging him to find out about the whereabouts of the families as quickly as possible. It was therefore a great relief for all of us when about a week later we heard the good news that they were still in Japan. Their departure from Japan for Russia had for unknown reasons been delayed and thus they were still safe and sound when the German-Russian conflict started.

Our camp returned to a kind of normalcy, except that everyone felt that the expanded war would indefinitely postpone the day of a cease-fire and with it also our return to freedom.

Suddenly a second bombshell hit us in that momentous year of 1941. On Monday, December 8 (Sunday, December 7, in Hawaii) we learned within a few hours after the event had occurred, that the Japanese had attacked Pearl Harbor from the air. Even without knowing how much damage the raid had done, we sensed at once that we were now entering a phase in the war that would involve us.

No longer did this great conflict rage thousands of miles from our isolated life in a remote jungle camp on an island in the Indian Ocean. The entrance into the war of the most powerful nation of East Asia changed all this. Within days not only the United States joined the gigantic struggle in Europe, but also America's overseas colony, the Philippines, and the colonies of Britain, the Netherlands, and France found themselves drawn into the war. Within days after the attack on Pearl Harbor the Japanese juggernaut moved toward and into the practically defenseless region to the south: the Philippines, Hong Kong, Malaysia, Indochina, and Thailand. That it would soon attack the Netherlands East Indies we all expected.

It was also clear to us that the Dutch would not want its German prisoners to fall into the hands of the Japanese for fear that we would not only cooperate with Japan as citizens of a power allied to her, but also that we might take revenge for the treatment we had received at the Onrust camp. We sensed right away that the colonial authorities would do everything possible to move us away from East Asia before Japan overran Sumatra. Therefore, it did not surprise us when a few days after the attack on Pearl Harbor we noticed unmistakable signs that some changes for us were in the making.

On December 21 we received the first official word of our imminent departure for a destination "away from the war zone." Soon thereafter we found a list on our announcement board containing the names of those who would leave the camp on the first transport the twenty-third of December. To my great disappointment I saw listed all my Adventist missionary colleagues plus the son of one of them, but my name was missing. It was, therefore, with sad feelings that we said goodbye to each other, not knowing where, when, and if we would meet again. I felt once more as if loved ones had been torn away from me.

Five days after their departure, the second list of names appeared.

This time my name was on it. I had already packed my boxes of books and my other few belongings, and on the morning of December 29 I loaded them on military trucks after a Dutch soldier inspected the contents of my suitcase and wooden boxes. The only item he confiscated was my driver's license, the last identification document I still possessed. So far I had always been able to conceal it during inspections. I was sad to lose it for I had not one document to identify myself.

When the truck left with the few earthly goods that I possessed, I voiced a silent prayer asking God to keep an eye on my books, papers, and the other things that meant so much to me in the conditions under which I lived. Some people may consider it childish for a grown man to expect God to watch over a few dozen books in a far-off corner of the world where every day goods worth many millions of dollars, and innumerable human lives, perished. Yet I possessed such a faith in God's omnipotence that I literally accepted Jesus' assurance that not a hair on my head would be lost without God's will or approval.

The only things that we could take with us on the transport were an empty kerosene canister, which each of us owned for the weekly laundry; a set of underwear; a towel and soap; and a plate, cup, and spoon. We could not have knives, forks, or any other tools, or paper, pens, or books of any kind. In other words, we found ourselves once more reduced to the conditions of the first two months of our internment.

The idea of having to travel for days or weeks in the hold of a ship or in closed moving vans and trucks without being able to shave, cut fingernails, or read, was not at all appealing. Consequently, we did not eagerly look forward to it, the more so since we had to cross oceans now part of the war zone. The dangers of hitting mines and being attacked by submarines or bombers from the air had become a reality.

The next morning we left our camp in Alas Valley. For months we had longed for this day and looked forward to it with keen anticipation. However, we had expected that we would go as free men. How different was our actual departure. We left a place surrounded by beautiful mountains and lush tropical forests, a place in which we had experienced some of the most gorgeous sunsets we had ever seen. But we had also lived in complete isolation. Here I had not seen a single female since I had arrived 17 months earlier, and here I had nearly died from tropical disease.

Once more I was lucky to be assigned to an open truck. Although the barbed wire strung over a wooden frame surrounded us, we could observe and admire the fantastic mountain scenery of northern Sumatra. Never having traveled this route before, it was all new to me and a pleasant change from the monotony of the past months. I thoroughly enjoyed the trip. Toward evening we reached the big city of Pematangsiantar, where the colonial authorities put us into a large jail that covered a good-sized city block. Except for convicts kept in solitary confinement, the entire prison population had moved to other quarters in the city to make space for us. Evidently we were considered much more dangerous than the run-of-the-mill criminals.

In the prison we found long barracks with straw on the floor. Soon someone discovered a message scratched, probably with a spoon, in the plaster of one of the walls. Written by one of the members of the first transport who had spent a night in the place several days before our arrival, it advised us to stay away from the straw, which contained all kinds of vermin. As a result, many of the internees decided to spend the night in the open courtyard.

Soon after our arrival the air raid sirens sounded an alarm, and we heard loudspeaker vans passing through the city urging all people to extinguish lights and open fires. However, the floodlights of our prison were not switched off, making us a perfect target for the Japanese aircraft. Nevertheless the target of the Japanese squadron was not the city of Pematangsiantar, but Medan, northern Sumatra's principal city, which that night suffered a heavy attack, as we learned the next day from one of the officers who accompanied us. In the meantime the prison kitchen provided us with a comparatively good meal while the internees killed time by singing all kinds of German folk songs, which the convicts in their cells on death row vigorously applauded. We thus had a grateful audience.

Regardless of the warning not to sleep in the barracks, a few of us, myself included, did so anyway. I knew from my travels in South Sumatra, where I had spent many a night in native huts, that vermin or insects, with the exception of mosquitoes and flies, do not bother me. I trusted my luck and slept really well. Next morning some of my friends told me that after sunrise, when they could see me in the barracks, they noticed I was sound asleep, oblivious to all kinds of things crawling over me.

During the second day of travel I was even luckier. For some reason I stood at the end of the hundreds of people waiting to board the trucks to continue their trip. The officers squeezed as many people as they could into each of the vehicles. As soon as a truck was filled, they closed it and sent it on its way. In the end only three or four internees remained in the prison courtyard. When we came outside, the guards discovered that so few of us were left that it would not pay to use a large truck for such a small number of prisoners. Therefore, they sent us back to the courtyard, where we waited for more than an hour wondering what they would do with us. When the gate opened again, they put us into a brand-new American station wagon, a completely normal passenger car with not an inch of barbed wire in evidence. With us was a driver, an officer, and a soldier to guard us. Off we went.

A trip made in style, it was something I had never expected would happen to me. It was the most comfortable ride in the six and a half years of my internment. In one village our car stopped at a wayside native restaurant and the officer allowed each of us singly to use the restroom. He bought drinks not only for himself, the soldier, and driver, but also for us. His behavior so amazed us that we hardly knew how to thank him. Since for more than a year and a half we had received frequent abuse and little understanding of our situation, we could hardly believe that this world still contained some decent people who could see a human individual in a citizen of an enemy nation.

Shortly before we reached the town of Tarutung that lies at picturesque Lake Toba our officer received word through his radio that a squadron of Japanese planes had been spotted flying in our direction. Our car immediately stopped, and the officer, driver, and soldier went into the dense jungle through which we were passing. The officer told us to stay in the car. If we would attempt to leave it, they would instantly shoot us. We never saw or heard any of the enemy planes, but felt uncomfortable being a defenseless target for any hostile aircraft that might spot our solitary automobile standing on the road. When we later passed through the town of Tarutung we saw its naval air station in ruins and all its seaplanes still in flames from the attack.

The remainder of the trip was most enjoyable. We passed through the Batakland, a Christian country. Here we saw a church in every village and viewed the peculiar architecture of the native population. The last part of our trip led us through a wild, romantic, and mountainous region. As the road took us over numerous hairpin curves to the low-lying coastal area of northwestern Sumatra, we had some most scenic vistas of that rich country.

In Sibolga our car stopped at a Chinese girls' school that housed a part of the second transport. The classrooms were already occupied as well as the roofed-over verandas, but I found a space underneath an overhanging roof where I could find some protection from the rainstorms that hit that part of the world almost every day. There we spent two long miserable days, including New Year's Day 1942, waiting for our ship to arrive. The meals were atrocious. The authorities had hired a Chinese caterer to feed us, and he was evidently out to get rich in a hurry. What we got was boiled rice three times a day. Brought to us in large kettles, it contained a tiny bit of cooked vegetables, called sayur, and enough meat to provide everyone with a piece the size of an American quarter. That our men extensively cursed the merchant together with his ancestors and offspring one can easily understand.

On the morning of January 2, 1942, we received word that our ship, the Dutch East Indies S.S. *Plancius,* had docked. Like all the ships that hauled passengers and goods between the hundreds of islands in the East Indies archipelago, the *Plancius* carried cabin and deck passengers, but also had large holds to transport cargo. After a thorough body frisking to make sure that we carried no contraband, the guards marched us to the harbor and we embarked. Our transport consisted of about 1,000 men distributed over the two empty holds of the ship. Before we descended into the holds, each of us received a rectangular cardboard with a string attached to it so we could hang it on the chest. Each of the boards had a number printed in large numerals on one side.

Entering the aft hold I noticed a number of men lying in one corner, none of whom I recognized. They turned out to be sick Germans, mostly old veterans, who had served in the Dutch East

Indies Army for many years. Some had tuberculosis, others were terminally ill from cancer or other diseases. The colonial government had taken them from veterans' hospitals and sanitariums in Java and other islands and put them on board in Djakarta. Their story of the voyage that already lay behind them was one of great hardship and suffering. Since the ship provided no nursing service for them and the makeshift toilet was located on deck, some had been able to climb up and down the stairway only with the help of other patients. It was a great relief for them to reach Sibolga where they received the meager help our doctors and young healthy men could provide under such primitive circumstances.

We soon found out that the available space was inadequate. It was hardly enough to allow every man to lie on his side, like sardines in a can. Those who had to get up during the night to reach the latrine on deck almost had to be contortionists to reach the stairway without stepping on someone. It was especially a nuisance for those lying near the stairway since any man who wanted to use the facilities on deck, could climb up only after he had identified himself in a loud voice and exactly categorized his call of nature to the armed soldier at the upper end of the stairway. There was almost always a commotion during the 10 nights we spent on board the ship.

As soon as the last man had reached our quarters, a lieutenant descended to our hold accompanied by two machine-gun-carrying soldiers. The officer, from whose belt hung a string of hand grenades, carried in his right hand a revolver, while he held in his left hand a typewritten sheet containing the rules we had to follow. Among them were regulations that governed the twice-daily roll calls. He told us that during each roll call we had to sit on the floor, cross-legged in numerical order, in rows with the numbered cardboards hanging from our necks so that he could read the numbers. From the moment he would enter until he would leave our quarters, every man had to sit immovable on the floor with both hands held at his back. Moving of any part of the body, including arms or hands, would be interpreted as an attempt to attack the military personnel and would immediately be answered by shooting.

We all knew that it was no hollow threat. Therefore we all took the warning seriously and gave no cause for an incident in our hold. This was not easy, because during a heavy sea one day some men, being seasick, had to throw up. Since they could not use their hands to catch their vomit, they involuntarily spewed it on their own and their neighbor's clothing. Later we learned that the men in the fore hold were less lucky or disciplined and triggered a shooting that fortunately only wounded two men.

The lack of a water faucet or any sanitary facilities in our quarters posed serious problems. The only water that we received came in large metal containers together with our meals. It sufficed for our drinking needs, but was not enough to wash our hands, not to mention the brushing of teeth. Even if we had had sufficient water for such purposes, we had no way of disposing of any waste water, since our hold was just like an iron box without any outlet except on top. There steel and canvas covers prevented both rain and sufficient fresh air from reaching us. Traveling in close quarters for days on end in a tropical sea, such as the Indian Ocean, kept us perspiring profusely much of the time. The air became so thick that one could almost cut it with a knife. One of our men claimed to have heard one soldier saying to another after a roll call, "Boy, these guys produce a strong stench—they stink!"

Another nuisance was the latrines. Since they could not be put into our holds, the ship's crew set up two such installations with canvas enclosures on the deck, one aft and the other on the fore deck. The guards allowed only three men at a time to use each of them during the day and one man at night. Therefore during daylight one had to stand in line, and the line was always a long one. Sailors frequently hosed all the human wastes into the sea.

Soon after our embarkation we heard the noise of iron chains being drawn over the deck above our heads. We knew that the crew had weighed anchor. Soon thereafter we left the harbor and sailed out into the open sea, not knowing in which direction we were going. Many of us hoped that Australia would be our destination since some knowledgeable internees claimed that Australia had treated German internees well during World War I, while the rumor went around that those who had at that time been imprisoned in India had not fared so well.

Once during the early part of our voyage we heard the guns installed on deck firing at something. We had seen them when we embarked in Sibolga. Now we did not know whether the crew was practicing or whether our ship was under attack. Therefore our spokesman requested to see the commanding officer of the detachment of soldiers who accompanied us. He asked him what we should do if our ship was attacked. The regulations announced to us said not a word about lifeboat drills or what we would have to do in an emergency. We were also apprehensive not knowing whether there were any life vests on board for us—more than 1,000 internees. The answer given was "In the case of an attack keep calm and quiet. If not, we have enough hand grenades on board to make you be quiet."

On the fifth day of our voyage our ship apparently entered a harbor. Through a little hole in the enclosure of the latrine someone claimed to have seen coconut palm trees, which suggested that we were probably at Colombo, Ceylon (now Sri Lanka). Evidently the crew discovered the hole and covered it from the outside so that we could see nothing during the few hours of our stay there.

After leaving what we believed to have been Colombo, we noticed within a day that the weather became cooler. We stopped perspiring and guessed that we were sailing in a northerly direction toward Bombay, which in January can be quite cool. On Friday afternoon, January 9, we entered a harbor that indeed turned out to be Bombay. All of us expected that we would disembark immediately. The sailors had already removed the covers from our holds. However, we were bitterly disappointed.

Some British health officers boarded the ship and climbed down into our hold. They had learned we had sick people among us. When they saw the men in their pitiful condition, they declared—as we later learned—that there would not be enough time to process the ship and its human cargo before the harbor quarantine facilities closed for the weekend. They therefore ordered the ship to sail back to sea and return on Monday morning, prolonging our ordeal for another two and a half days. It meant that we would have to suffer through six more of the abominable roll calls on board ship, to sleep three more nights in cramped positions, to stand in line again to get to the latrine, and last but not least, to eat eight more of the inadequate and tasteless meals, which we had already endured for nearly two weeks.

While the days had seemed indescribably long during the voyage to India, we now felt that they would never end. Yet even they eventually came to an end. Monday morning arrived, and while we steamed slowly back into the Bombay harbor, sailors once more removed the steel and canvas covers of our holds and let fresh air and sunshine enter.

The first people taken off were the sick. Medics entered our hold and helped those who could walk to reach the deck while the others left on stretchers were lifted out of the hold by a crane. Evidently they went to a local or military hospital. We never saw them again. I have no idea how many of them, if any, survived the war.

For some reason we did not leave the ship until late in the afternoon. At noon each one of us received with his boiled rice and vegetables an extra-large portion of fish, more than we needed. It surprised us, but we ate it all since we had no containers or bags to save it. Later we learned that it was also supposed to serve as our evening meal.

It was a happy occasion when we disembarked from the S.S. *Plancius*. For us it had been like a real slave ship, except that we were not, as the Black cargo of the seventeenth- or eighteenth-century slave ships, transported in chains.

At once we noticed that the Gurkha troops, who now guarded us, held their guns so that the muzzles pointed to the sky, while the East Indies soldiers always pointed their weapons at us whenever they had to accompany us. This we interpreted as a friendly gesture; others soon followed. The Gurkhas led us into a large empty godown where a British officer addressed us as "gentlemen," a term we had not heard for more than 20 months. He apologized that he had no chairs or benches to offer us to sit on, and explained that our waiting time would not be long. We would soon be able to sit in railway cars. At the same time our captors served us tea with milk and sugar, according to British custom. Our first impression was good. In fact, we began to like our new enemy, but wondered whether our favorable impression would last.

Soon a long empty train arrived, and we boarded low-class carriages of the Indian railroad system. Each compartment contained two sleeping platforms, one above the other, but we had ample space for each of us to stretch out and sleep on the simple military mattresses we received. The windows were halfway open allowing us to see the passing scenery, but they were not open wide enough to let a man escape. Each car was guarded by two armed Gurkhas.

Before it grew dark we passed through the large metropolis of Bombay with its teeming millions. Since it was the time of the late-afternoon rush hour, the masses of people we saw on the streets as well as on the suburban trains overwhelmed us. The commuter trains were not only filled with passengers until no one else could possibly be squeezed in; they carried many sitting on the roofs and hanging like bunches of grapes on doors and windows outside the carriages. All was new to me, and I soaked the impressions in like a dry sponge. I only regretted that we would pass through the Western Ghats, the rugged, mountainous stretch of country between the coastal area and the highland, during the night and therefore could not enjoy the most scenic part of our journey.

Our train ride across the Indian subcontinent lasted four nights and three days. We passed through many villages and some large cities such as Nagpur, Bilaspur, and Rourkela. The colorful Indian country life fascinated me, for it differed in many respects from that which I had known in the East Indies. Since we saw something new all the time, the long trip was not boring at all. The British also took good care of us. From time to time the train halted for tea breaks. Our accompanying soldiers boiled the tea in large kettles over open fires. Our food consisted of bread, butter, and canned goods such as marmalade and jam, cheese, sardines, and corned mutton. For the first time I did not hear my fellow internees curse our wardens, jailers, guards, or the authorities.

Eventually we reached the Ranchi Junction station. I knew where we were since I had known a German nurse, the sister of one of my classmates in the Friedensau Missionary Seminary, who had served in a Seventh-day Adventist clinic at Ranchi. Our train spent the night there on a sidetrack and headed for Ramgarh on the Damodar River the next morning. From there we walked to our new camp, a distance of perhaps two miles. Those handicapped or who preferred a ride rode in army trucks.

As we passed several wings of the large camp before reaching the empty ones assigned to us, we saw our colleagues of the first transport who had reached the camp several days earlier. After a few days we Adventist internees obtained permission to move to the same wing. It made it possible to resume our weekly get-togethers for Bible studies and discussions.

Shortly after our arrival at Ramgarh the camp photographed each one of us and compared our identity with the ships' manifest. The administration discovered that a Siegfried Horn was not on the list the Dutch authorities had provided. Instead it contained an Ernest Horn, who had not arrived. It became obvious that I had joined the wrong transport and had been on the wrong ship. However, the mistake seemed to have caused no harm, since we assumed that the Ernest Horn would arrive with the third transport.

One day after another passed, and we heard nothing about the third transport. Many of our people became impatient and even apprehensive, since many men who had been on the second transport had not yet received their luggage that obviously had been loaded on the third ship. Furthermore, we had several young men with us whose fathers were on the third transport and some older men whose sons had not yet arrived. All our inquiries at the commandant's office brought no satisfactory reply. He had received word from his superiors to have facilities ready for another 1,000 internees, but he did not know when they would arrive.

Then on February 2, 1942, the *Statesman,* a Calcutta newspaper that we received daily, contained the following 10-line item:

"London, Jan. 31.

"Most of the Germans in the internment camp of Kotatjane in northern Sumatra are being sent to British India away from the war zone, it is learned from authoritative sources here.

"The last transport carrying internees was attacked by the Japanese, a great many casualties being caused, it is officially announced."

While I mourned for those who had lost their lives, I thanked my heavenly Father for saving me from a watery grave somewhere in the Indian Ocean.

I was now concerned that Jeanne know I was safe and sound in India, for I did not know whether she had received any news of the transfer of the German internees from Sumatra. We Adventists had already written to the Southern Asia Division office in Poona, India, and requested the officers there to notify the General Conference in

Washington, D.C., that we had all arrived safely.

A few weeks later I received a disturbing letter from Paul Bradley in the United States. He was, at the outbreak of the Japanese conflict, the secretary of the Far Eastern Division in Singapore. Before that city fell to the Japanese forces, Bradley had left for Java, where he stayed for several weeks until he obtained passage to Australia as one of the last Americans able to escape from Java before the Japanese occupied the island.

While Mr. Bradley was still in Djakarta, Jeanne received word from the Red Cross that the list of the German internees on the third transport contained my name, and it was assumed that I had perished when the Japanese sank the ship in the Indian Ocean. Bradley personally went to the Red Cross office in Djakarta to obtain further news, but the agency knew no particulars about the loss of the S.S. *Van Imhoff* and had nothing else but the ship's manifest, namely the list of the prisoners aboard it.

When Bradley arrived in America a few weeks after his escape from Java, he reported that we German Seventh-day Adventist missionaries had been transferred to India and that it seemed that all of us had safely arrived there except Siegfried Horn, who, according to the list of prisoners received from the Dutch authorities by the Red Cross, had lost his life when the Japanese destroyed his ship.

In this way I knew that Jeanne now consider herself a widow. I only hoped that some of my weekly cards sent to her would reach her in spite of the fact that we never received messages from our loved ones in the East Indies during the years of the Asiatic war and therefore had no certainty that they received any of our mail. Later we learned that the Japanese had closed that country so tightly that no messages of any kind went in or out for more than three and a half years. I asked my mother in Berlin, with whom I had regularly corresponded through the Red Cross, to contact the Japanese embassy in Berlin and request it to send word to Jeanne that I was safe and sound in India.

Not one of the various attempts to let her know that I was still alive was successful. It was not until the Japanese surrendered that she finally learned the truth. This was not simply a surprise for her—it was a real shock. The wounds produced by my alleged death had healed in the course of years, and she had to rethink her future.

Chapter VI

In India—East, West, and North

I will sketch only briefly the more than four and a half years I spent in three different prison camps in India, since they lacked the excitement and tragedy of the first two years of my internment. Except that the climatic conditions in each camp differed sharply from one to the other, our lifestyle varied little.

The first camp, in which we spent only six months, was at Ramgarh in the state of Bihar. It was located at the Damodar River, about 200 miles northwest of Calcutta. Because of a drought, we never had enough water for all our needs. The four wings occupied by our 2,000 German civilian internees formed only a small appendix to the huge camp complex that held some 60,000 Italian prisoners of war captured by the British during their military campaigns in and occupation of Eritrea, Ethiopia, Italian Somaliland, and Libya.

This camp allowed us to take brief walks on our word of honor not to make any attempts to escape. It gave us a wonderful feeling to stroll along and swim in the Damodar River with no armed soldier guarding us or pointing a gun at us. The facility had a movie house to which those who wanted could occasionally go in groups to see a movie.

We also had the privilege of accepting money from the outside. Those who had bank accounts in neutral countries could draw from them, while others, like we Adventist missionaries, who had been employed by an American or other Allied organization, could receive financial support from such bodies. We requested that the Southern Asia Division obtain financial assistance from the General Conference for us. The denomination granted our request, and after a while regular financial aid arrived. It helped us to purchase from our camp canteen diary products such as eggs and cheese, since we frequently could not eat what the camp kitchen provided (pork, lard, ham, and sausage formed a large part of the daily menu).

Since we could also purchase other merchandise as long as it was manufactured in India, I ordered and received a camp stool, a folding table, and a wooden bookshelf. These items made it possible for me to continue my studies without interruption right at my bedside. I had found studying in the dining halls difficult because the noisy card players were such a nuisance most of the time. Furthermore, I had to vacate my study table when mealtime began. Later I bought myself a secondhand typewriter.

For some imported quality products we depended on supplies smuggled into the camp. The regulations against such items had been issued since it did not seem fair to the authorities to provide us, citizens of an enemy nation, with goods and products brought into the country by Allied sailors who had risked their lives to do so. During the war the india ink and paper I had been forced to use were of inferior quality. Thus, I was most happy when good American writing paper and Skrip ink became available, although at exorbitant prices. For a bottle of imported ink I had to pay the equivalent of five dollars in rupees, and that in 1943 dollars.

Our camp commandant knew what was going on, but evidently tolerated such minor infractions of the camp rules and regulations to keep the atmosphere peaceful and quiet. Yet he wanted us to know that he was aware of the fact that the Indian merchants who supplied our camp store with permitted products and merchandise also smuggled in imported goods for which they charged us high prices to cover their risks. One day the commandant, a British colonel, appeared in our canteen and asked for a can of Australian cheese. The canteen clerk, one of our fellow internees, replied, "Sir, I can sell you only local cheeses. You know that we are not permitted to have imported products." The commandant then retorted, "You better get me what I asked, or I will bring my soldiers into your shop and take the wanted cheese without paying for it." He got his cheese and paid the high price that the merchant had charged us.

We will remember the camp at Ramgarh especially for a most frightening experience we had there. One afternoon a black column that seemed to reach from the earth to the sky raced toward our camp. Within minutes a sandstorm blew over us with a howling ferocity and intensity that only those who have ever been in the path of a tornado can understand. It sounded as if a dozen freight trains hurtled through our camp at the same time. We had closed all doors and window shutters and prayed that our barracks would be able to withstand the force. In the meantime it had become as dark as night, and fine sand penetrated all openings so that as we stood inside our barracks we inhaled it into our lungs in spite of the handkerchiefs that we held over our nostrils.

The sandstorm lasted only seconds, but it left a path of destruction from one end of our camp to the other. Our wing and many others had suffered little damage, but those wings that had been right in the center of the tornado's path had had roofs ripped off and latrine and shower sheds destroyed. Even a water tower had been plucked up from its moorings and hurled on the grounds of a football field. It seemed a miracle that no one was killed or seriously injured.

However, we had a formidable cleaning job on our hands. Fine-grained sand covered everything. A layer of dust covered beds, books, clothing, even the insides of suitcases. It took us many hours to get all our belongings clean again while for days we coughed up brown dust that we had involuntarily inhaled.

As the summer of 1942 approached, the Japanese forces had already overrun large parts of Burma and were nearing the eastern border of India. The authorities had to reckon with the possibility that even the Indian province of Bengal might fall into the hands of the enemy. For that reason the British decided to ship the Italian POWs to America and the German internees to Deoli, a camp in the western part of India that the colony had used in the past for political prisoners. Later we learned that the Ramgarh camp served after our departure as a base and training camp for Allied forces shipped into eastern India to fight against the Japanese invaders.

After six months at the Ramgarh camp we traveled by train to Deoli in Rajputana, western India. Our three-day-and-night ride took us through the holy city of Benares (Varanasi) on the Ganges River, also through Allahabad and Agra to Kotah. We were disappointed that we failed to see the world-famous Taj Mahal at Agra since it was at midnight during a moonless night that we crossed the Yamuna River over a railroad bridge. The Taj Mahal is clearly visible during daytime from this bridge. Kotah, which lies on the trunk line between Delhi and Bombay, was the railroad station where we had to exchange the train for army trucks to take us to our camp at Deoli, some 50 miles to the west.

I volunteered to ride on top of one of the trucks filled with luggage. From this vantage point I watched the desertlike countryside through which we traveled. It was a real treat that we drove through Bundi, the capital of a small maharaja-ruled state, which is idyllically nestled in a natural depression of the hilly country through which we passed. The picturesque and colorful palace of the maharaja built in the typical Indian style looked like a jewel in the dry country that surrounded it.

Our first impression of the new camp was a good one. It seemed to us that the barracks with their thick, whitewashed walls and flat roofs were solid structures that would remain comfortably cool during the hot summer months. They also provided us with plenty of space, more than we had ever had before, while large windows gave us all the light we wanted. That their appearance was deceptive we learned later.

Just as we had an unusual experience in Ramgarh during our six-month stay in east India when a devastating tornado swept through our camp, Deoli provided us with one of a different kind— an uncommon and unheralded rainstorm. The usual annual rainfall in Deoli amounts to about eight inches. But in August 1942 a rainstorm visited our area and shed 36 inches of rain on Deoli in just five days.

At first we were happy when the rains started. It was practically the first we had experienced in India since our arrival seven months earlier. However, the rain soon came down in sheets transforming our camp, which lacked any drainage system, into a muddy lake. The next thing we noticed was that our flat roofs began to leak. Since, as we later learned, they consisted of a three-foot-thick mixture of clay, dirt, and cow dung, any rainwater that seeped through became brown, muddy water. First we shifted our beds and belongings to dry spots. I moved at least three times within my barracks before I had to flee to safety outside. The walls and roof began to disintegrate and the first wooden ceiling beam crushed down.

Helping each other, we carried our belongings through the raging flood to the dining hall and kitchen structure, which was built of solid, fire-baked bricks. That building also rested on a high foundation and had a gabled metal roof. I was lucky that my barracks was one of the first that began to collapse, thus forcing us to flee to the only safe building in our wing before the general exodus from all barracks began. Finding a refuge on the roofed-over outside veranda of the dining hall, we stashed our soaked mattresses and other belongings on the floor.

Soon the occupants of other barracks followed suit, telling us how the ceiling beams were collapsing, as well as the wooden windowsills and doorframes. However, unlike us, they were not so lucky as we had been in finding dry spaces to sleep. For them the soldiers who guarded us moved army tents into the compounds and pitched them in the muddy sport fields inside the wings. The sleeping accommodations in army tents, in which the beds stood in four inches of water, were far from pleasant. Within a day or so it looked as if a squadron of Flying Fortresses had bombed our camp and thoroughly destroyed all buildings except the dining hall and kitchen structure.

Our barracks had been built of sun-dried mudbricks. The three-foot-thick walls were covered on the inside and outside by a layer of whitewashed plaster. The ceiling consisted of wooden beams spread with mats. On top of the mattings lay the thick layer of clay, dirt, and cow dung pressed down by stone rollers. A thin layer of mud plaster put over it made such a roof quite waterproof for the normal conditions of infrequent and light showers. However, this type of structure could not withstand a five-day torrential rainstorm, a storm that area of India experiences only once in 100 years. It just happened that it occurred during our nine-month stay there.

As soon as the storm had passed, the sun quickly dried the muddy ground in our compounds and within days the reconstruction of our barracks, bath houses, and latrines began. One morning we saw hundreds of villagers—men, women, children, and infants—entering our wing. Accompanied by millions of flies, they carried simple tools, baskets, and their lunches.

First the mothers secured their babies so that they could not crawl away or get lost. They rammed wooden pegs into the ground, attached a short string to each one of them and fastened the other end to the legs of their naked infants. The mothers returned from time to time to nurse them, but otherwise left them all day long to their own fate. Most of the time the children slept. The hot sun did not seem to bother or hurt them, nor did the multitude of flies that settled around their mouths, nostrils, eyes, and ears. It seemed that the infants had been born with a tolerance to the pests that bothered us so much.

The villagers were all experts in constructing the type of buildings in which we had lived. Hauling cartloads of cow dung into the camp, they mixed it with water and the debris of our collapsed buildings and shaped the mud into rather large rectangular bricks, which they spread out on the ground to dry in the sun. As soon as the bricks hardened, the reconstruction of the walls began. The villagers set the doors and window frames back into the walls, and reset those old roof beams that had not broken when they came crushing down under the load of dirt and rain. New mattings over the wooden beams held up the thick layer of roofing mixture. A whitewashed layer of plaster inside and outside on all walls completed the building. Incredibly, they rebuilt the whole camp in just a few weeks, after which it showed no signs of its former ruinous state. If Deoli would not have another unusual rainfall, the barracks, knowledgeable people informed us, could survive 20 or more years.

At the time of our arrival in Deoli the officials told us that we would stay only a short time since a more permanent camp was under construction at Dehra Dun in the foothills of the Himalayan Mountains. As one month after another passed without any definite announcement of a departure date, we feared that we might get stuck for a long time in this desert with its extremely hot summers and rainless seasons that left us always short of water so that we never had enough for showering and laundering.

What we deplored more than anything else were the latrines to which the native population had evidently become used to. They had neither a sewer nor a drainage system, and consisted of cells with wooden seats. Under each seat stood a low rectangular metal container that "sweepers"—low-caste Indians—emptied daily. Although the authorities had some lime put into the containers regularly, they spread a disgusting odor and seemed to be the principal breeding ground of the millions of flies that pestered us unmercifully.

I could study only by sitting underneath a mosquito net. It protected me at night from the mosquitoes and during the day from the flies. We actually took our food from the dining hall with us to our barracks during the summer when the fly plague was worst, and ate our meals while sitting underneath the nets. Those who did not do it always needed one hand to chase the flies away from both food and mouth. Never could I understand better than in the desertlike area of Deoli in western India why the ancients worshiped a god of the flies, Beelzebub, whom they tried to appease by sacrifices.

We attempted to exterminate the flies by catching them in bottles. At various spots in our barracks we placed empty bottles, into which we poured some sweet tea. The tea attracted the flies, which then flew or crawled into the bottles and drowned. Their corpses produced fermentation. Its odor became even more attractive to the insects and lured them into the bottles by the hundreds and thousands every day. We had to empty the bottles at least every other day, but always left some residue of the fermented cadavers at the bottom as a bait for the next generation of flies.

Another complaint our men had was the lack of sufficient protein in our diet, by which they meant meat. The British officials told us that we received the amount of meat by weight to which each internee was entitled. However, the meat included the bones. Every morning ox-drawn carts arrived filled with the carcasses of emaciated desert goats. The goats contained such minuscule amounts of meat that the bones shipped out of our camp weighed almost as much as the original animals. The camp commandant said that he sympathized with us, but told us, that it was also the chief complaint of the British soldiers who served under his command. The Gurkhas and the native soldiers seemed to be satisfied with the situation.

Twice during our stay in Deoli he arranged for beef for our camp. He had to do it in utter secrecy, he explained, because the population in that part of India was so fanatical, that when a previous camp commandant had brought in beef for the British soldiers, he had a riot on his hands that could be suppressed only through force. It earned him a demotion in rank, since he should have known that he could not, with impunity, injure the religious feelings of the Hindus of his area, who considered the slaughter of cattle a major crime.

What our commandant did on the two occasions when he managed to smuggle beef into our camp was to send trucks, driven by British drivers, to Karachi, a predominantly Muslim city, where they bought beef from which all the bones had been removed, and drove it to Deoli. They timed the arrival of the trucks so that they would reach the camp after dark. In this way the local population could not see what they hauled. Our cooks and many helpers, recruited from the internees, worked feverishly all night to convert the beef into sausages and cooked steaks, so that the Indian sweepers, who would enter the camp the next morning, would not discover the beef. Since the non-Indian officers and soldiers were just as keen to have a change of diet as our internees were and were to receive their share of the beef-containing products, the ruse worked and no religious feelings were hurt.

After about nine months the commandant announced the dates of our departure to the new camp in Dehra Dun. However, before we actually left, a sad mixup occurred. It resulted from a breakdown of communication between our camp administration and its higher-ups in the Delhi government, over the arrival of new inmates. The episode caused a lot of ill feelings among our internees and also between us and the administration. The government had decided to make the Deoli camp an internment camp for Japanese women and their children and they suddenly showed up by the hundreds while we still occupied the camp. Our commandant claimed that he had received word of their coming only a day before the first transport actually reached us. To make room for them the internees of two of our four wings had to move into the other two wings, greatly overcrowding them.

I and some of my missionary friends suddenly found ourselves in another wing, which within hours had doubled its population. That we were not greeted with open arms is understandable. Almost intolerable conditions of overcrowding were created. We had to leave our beds behind, and the kitchen did not have enough pots and pans or working space for double the number of cooks, or enough stoves to feed us all at one sitting. Also the latrines that were hardly enough to meet the needs of 500 people had suddenly to serve 1,000. As a result tempers flared over trivial things.

The worst results of hundreds of women, separated from us by only a 10-foot-wide no-man's-land and two barbed-wire fences, was the arousal of passions among many of the male inmates in our camp. After all they had not been around any women for nearly three years. It was interesting to see the Japanese women arriving, many with children of all ages, and to talk through the barbed-wire fences to those who spoke English. We listened eagerly to the stories of their experiences since their internment had started more than a year before. No one interfered with such conversations.

But the situation became nasty during the first night, as I learned the next morning. Some of our young men had found out that the hundreds of Japanese women and children included prostitutes. They crawled underneath the fences and through the no-man's-land into the neighboring Japanese wings. There they not only visited the prostitutes but also molested some married women. In general, the Japanese women were disgusted with the behavior of our men, and their leaders talked with our leaders through the fences the next morning and requested them to restrain their men. Since the Japanese and the Germans were on the same side in the war, it seemed abhorrent to them to seek the help from the British administration—protection by their enemy from their allies.

Unfortunately the traffic of our men to the wings of the women increased during the second night. It forced the Japanese leaders to call upon the British authorities to put a stop to it, which they attempted to do by placing sentries in the no-man's-land every few yards. In spite of such measures the unsavory visits continued during the third night.

The Japanese women, who now patrolled their own wings, turned over to the British authorities several men who in spite of all warnings and the increased number of sentries had still managed to get into the women's wings. The commandant sentenced them to several weeks of solitary confinement, putting them for the first week on a diet of dry bread and water. When we left a few days later the men traveled with us, but on arrival in Dehra Dun had to complete their punishment in the cell block of the new camp. The commandant of the Deoli camp told our wing leaders that he was so disgusted by the behavior of so many of our internees, that he sentenced them to the maximum punishment he was allowed to mete out, and would have gladly increased it if he had had the authority to do so.

Our departure from Deoli left a bitter taste in the mouth of all parties involved: the Japanese women, the British camp administration, and the majority of the German internees, decent men who strongly condemned the acts of some of their fellow internees.

On the other hand we were more than happy when the day of departure came as it released us from the intolerable overcrowding in our two wings. We also looked forward to a camp that had been described to us as being located in ideal surroundings and a pleasant climate, where we would have all the water we wanted year around. Thus it was with great expectation that we left our fourth camp in three years of imprisonment.

Our three-day trip to our fifth camp took us first by army trucks and buses to Kota, and from there by train to Dehra Dun with a six-hour layover at the railway station of Delhi. In Delhi we had to change trains and were, during the few hours of waiting, molested by a minor sandstorm. Otherwise the journey was uneventful and a pleasant change from the monotonous and somewhat austere and uncomfortable life in the desert.

The south-north railway from Bombay to Delhi and beyond ends in Dehra Dun, a city situated at an elevation of about 2,000 feet in the foothills of the majestic Himalayan Mountains. The Himalayas rise steeply right behind the city. Dehra Dun enjoys a pleasant climate all year with no extreme temperatures either in the summer or in the winter, although snow falls occasionally.

At Dehra Dun an internment camp for German civilians had already existed for three years when we arrived. In contrast to those of us from the East Indies who had in most cases no more than a suitcase or less, the German internees who had moved into this camp at the beginning of the war with some of their own furniture, all their books, radios, record players, pictures, tables, and bed linens seemed to us to live in luxury.

A few weeks after our arrival I visited an Adventist missionary whom I had known as a fellow college student in Friedensau. He took me to a restaurant in his wing and ordered a meal for both of us. Surprised by what I saw, I remained speechless for several minutes. Here I sat on a regular chair at a normal table covered with a white tablecloth and ate from fine china and drank out of a glass as in prewar years. A waiter dressed in white served the meal.

I learned that the internees had brought everything from their former homes and that many wealthy internees could draw on their bank accounts. This enabled them to employ fellow internees who had no outside resources as waiters, cooks, or kitchen helpers, or in other menial work.

The contrast of life between that wing and ours was enormous. We ate at long tables fashioned from rough wooden boards and sat on equally primitive benches, had neither tablecloths nor vases of flowers on our tables, and ate from metal plates and drank from the metal mugs we had received in our first camp on the island of Onrust.

The four wings for the German internees from the Dutch East Indies had been added to those already existing when the rapid Japanese advance during the spring and summer of 1942 threatened eastern India and made our removal from that area advisable. The barracks in the Dehra Dun camp had brick walls and gabled thatch roofs. The open fireplaces were a novelty, with every barrack having several. We needed them during the winter months when cold winds and sometimes even snow swept down from the Himalayan Mountains.

During our stay on the island of Onrust and in the wild jungles of northern Sumatra the authorities never allowed us to leave the camp without heavily armed guards. This changed as soon as we arrived in India. We received permission to go off for several hours once a week both at Ramgarh as well as at Deoli. In Ramgarh we usually walked along and swam in the Damodar River, and in Deoli we hiked to a nearby small lake were we could also swim.

The commandant warned us that the privilege would be permanently withdrawn if anyone tried to use it to escape. To my knowledge no internee ever broke his word of honor during such excursions, although it frequently happened that some men miscalculated the distance they could cover in the allotted time, and consequently arrived too late at the place of assembly to be returned to the camp. Those who made such unfortunate mistakes always had to spend time in the cellblock, the length depending on how long they had overstayed their allowed time. Because of the summer heat in Ramgarh and Deoli, only a limited number of internees used the privilege to make extensive tours, but in the cooler months we took advantage of the opportunity to get out of our barbed-wire enclosures as often as we could and enjoyed a kind of imagined freedom.

In Dehra Dun, however, the weekly excursions became real highlights of our captivity. We soon learned that in the cool season we could make exciting day trips into the mountains to the north and south of our camp. An excursion to the north offered us panoramic views of a whole chain of the Himalayan Mountains, all perpetually covered by snow and ice.

On the other hand, the trips to the Siwalik Hills in the south took us to some of the oldest mountain formations in the world. Their strangely rugged ridges and unusually shaped peaks gave us the impression of having landed on the moon. Many years later I learned during a visit to the museum in Calcutta that no other mountainous area in India provides the paleozoologists with so many prehistoric, fossilized animal bones as the Siwalik Hills. In fact, the first postage stamp ever to depict a prehistoric animal—in this case the *Stegodon ganesa,* a long-tusked primeval elephant whose bones came from the Siwaliks—was issued in 1951 at the centennial of the Geological Survey of India.

However, to enjoy the mountain scenery required a training period that lasted for several weeks. We could view the Himalayas in all their splendor from two different summits. One was Cloud's End, a few miles west of Mussoorie, a famous hill-station of northern India, and the other was Mount Badraj, a mountain farther to the west. Their elevations were, respectively, 5,085 feet and 5,079 feet above our camp. The distance from our camp to Cloud's End as well as to Mount Badraj amounted to about 16 miles in a straight line with a difference of more than 5,000 feet in altitude. It meant that to make it to the top of one of the mountains we had to cover about 33 miles of which the outbound trip was almost a constant climb. For the training trips we had eight hours at our disposal, but for the days when we wanted to reach the top of one of the mountains we could apply for an extra one and a half hours.

I was determined to make it. At the age of 35 my chances of

success looked good. As soon as the cool season began, I started to get in shape. Each week I went a little farther and higher. Finally the memorable day came when on December 9, 1943, I reached Cloud's End. On that summit I had an incredible and unforgettable view. Before me stretched out a chain of 18 glacier-and-snow-covered mountains, none less than 20,000 feet. Nanda Devi with an elevation of 25,644 feet was the highest of all. Looking at my watch I knew I could spend only 20 minutes soaking in the marvelous view before I had to start the return journey. The view made me forget all the muscle aches and fatigue I had endured for weeks.

Then I tore myself away and descended, jumping from rock to rock, and running as fast as I could to reach the assembly point on time. A few times I nearly fainted from fatigue and thought that my knees would buckle. But then came a time when suddenly my strength seemed to return and the last mile was not so bad at all. Dead tired but extremely happy, I reached our wing.

During that winter I managed with some further training also to climb to the top of Mount Badraj. Although that summit is not higher than Cloud's End, it takes more time and energy to reach it since one has to cross several valleys. Eventually I even got to both mountain tops on the same day. I climbed first to the summit of Mount Badraj, and from there via a four-mile ridge over to Cloud's End and return, all in nine and a half hours. Since only a few men in our wing were able to do it, I was exceedingly proud of my accomplishment.

In the East Indies no one ever tried to escape since all internees knew that the chances of success were practically nil. Those who contemplated an attempt could also expect the death sentence, as threatened in the camp regulations, if recaptured.

In India the situation was different. In one of our wing commander's earliest speeches, he discouraged us from thinking of escape. He said that the chances of success in that gigantic Indian subcontinent were so slim and the hardships so great, that everyone should think twice before venturing out of the security of our camp. Notwithstanding such warnings someone attempted to escape at least once every month and sometimes more frequently.

It was not too difficult to crawl unseen by the sentries through or underneath the coils of the barbed-wire fences, but the hardships experienced outside were usually so tremendous that most men gave themselves up to the authorities within a few days. I know of one man shot dead by a sentry as he passed through no-man's-land between the two fences, while another man was murdered by villagers. His travel companion then surrendered to the police. Of some escapees we never heard anything after they disappeared and therefore do not know what happened to them. Many others were caught somewhere in that large country of India after having experienced untold hardships. When they returned from their adventure they preferred the security of camp life over that of a hounded fugitive.

Only two attempts succeeded. Mr. Heins Von Have, who had been my barracks leader in the Sumatra camp, together with a friend, jumped out of the train transporting us from the Ramgarh camp to the one in Deoli. They managed to get as far as Cox Bazar, south of Chittagong in eastern Bengal, less than 100 miles from the Japanese lines in Burma, their goal. However, British military policemen discovered them and transported them to Deoli, where they spent several weeks in cells before returning to our camp.

Several weeks later Von Have and his friend escaped again, this time from our camp. Early the next morning they flagged down a bus, hoping that they could get away before the first roll call would reveal their absence. The bus stopped for them and the two men boarded. As they started to take seats they noticed to their consternation that the British commander of our wing was sitting in the same bus. When Von Have saw him he immediately jumped out of the moving bus. His companion followed, but fell and hit his head on a rock. He suffered a broken skull and died from his injuries within minutes. Von Have who saw from a distance what had happened surrendered at once.

Still Von Have was not willing to give up, and within weeks he and Rolf Magener, another friend, were missed at the morning roll call. We wondered how far they would get this time. For more than two years we heard nothing about them until toward the end of the war one of our internees received through the Red Cross organization a brief letter from his wife in Japan. In it she told him that she had just listened to a lecture in the German club presented by Von Have about his experiences in India and Burma. This gave us proof that he had really succeeded in working his way through India and the British and Japanese frontlines. Only years later when I read the book *Prisoners' Bluff,* by Rolf Magener (New York: E. P. Dutton and Co., Inc., 1955), which describes the incredible adventures of the two escapees, did I learn of the enormous hardships they had passed through and what unexpected risks they had taken to slip undetected first through Allied lines and then through the Japanese lines.

In fact, when they finally surrendered to the Japanese their most dangerous period started. The Japanese soldiers and officers alike were embarrassed that anyone had succeeded in slipping undetected through their forces. Therefore, several times they almost executed the two men to hide the embarrassing incident from higher military authorities. Furthermore, they seriously considered the possibility that the two Germans were Allied spies. As a result Von Have and Magener spent months in Japanese jails before they could clear their names and authenticate their claims of being bona fide escaped German internees of the British. Eventually the Imperial forces sent them to Japan where their odyssey ended.

The other two men who made a successful escape came from one of the wings that housed Germans who had been interned in India. Both men, Heinrich Harrer and Peter Aufschnaiter, had been members of the German Himalaya expedition who happened to be in India when the war broke out. One of them, Harrer, had already made a name for himself before the war as the first mountaineer who had successfully climbed the north wall of the Eiger in Switzerland, previously considered unconquerable. In contrast to Von Have and Magener, Harrer and Aufschnaiter planned to cross the Himalayan Mountains with the aim of reaching Tibet. Like the other two successful escapees they experienced extreme hardships but of a different kind. Their greatest enemies were the cruel forces of nature and hostile Tibetan officials and citizens. Despite the fact that they lacked the necessary clothing and sufficient financial resources, they crossed mountain passes more than 17,000 feet above sea level and traveled on foot at high altitudes for many hundreds of miles before they reached Tibet's capital, Lhasa, one and a half years after leaving the camp at Dehra Dun. Somehow Harrer succeeded in befriending high officials in Lhasa and became acquainted with the young Dalai Lama, whose tutor he eventually became. He stayed with the Dalai Lama for several years after the war, until the invading Chinese forced him and the young Tibetan ruler to flee. Harrer describes his adventures in the book *Seven Years in Tibet* (London: Rupert Hart-Davis, 1953).

Chapter VII

Free at Last

Ever since we had received newspapers in Sumatra we all followed the global struggle with unceasing interest. We learned during the early war years of the reverses and gains, defeats and victories of the Allied powers, and to a lesser degree of the Axis forces. After 1943 the tide turned. It became obvious to anyone but the blind that the armed forces of the Axis nations were no longer holding their own but were slipping, first from offensive to defensive positions, and soon thereafter retreating on all fronts.

However, it was unwise to voice defeatest thoughts in our camps for fear of punishment by the fanatical Nazis in our midst. Occasionally someone made a careless remark and as a result received bad beatings from hooded assailants at night. One man awoke as a barrel of human waste was poured over his head, while another had his bed set on fire while he slept. Although the camp authorities in Sumatra as well as in India did not tolerate such acts and usually punished them by closing the canteen, cinema, and sportsfield, and by retracting the privilege of excursions until the culprits would be found or their names be revealed, I do not know of one case in which they were actually discovered. Each time the authorities relented after a while and allowed the camp shop to reopen, the sports activities to resume, and the visits to the camp cinema and the weekly excursions to begin again.

Even three months before the end of the war in Europe, most internees did not dare to say aloud what everyone knew, namely that Germany as well as Japan were rushing headlong into terrible national catastrophes.

And then the end came almost overnight. Partisans executed Mussolini April 28, and his friend Hitler died by his own hand in the ruins of Berlin several days later. German forces capitulated within days, and the Japanese three months after that. We read about the great victory celebrations in London and many other cities in Europe and America when the European war ended, and in New York and all over the world when the Asiatic war ceased.

Also we learned of the survivors of the bestial Nazi death camps and of the Allied prisoners of war who regained their freedom after having suffered in German or Japanese camps. But no one ever mentioned the German and Japanese military POWs or civilian internees. It seemed to us that we belonged to a forgotten race.

The newspapers told about protest marches made at the White House in Washington, D.C., and toward the House of Parliament in London with their banners demanding, "Bring the boys home!" The repatriation of the hundreds of thousands of service men spread all over the world could not be carried out quickly because of the lack of sufficient ships or other transport facilities. It is understandable that their loved ones, fathers and mothers, wives and sweethearts, became impatient with the slow progress.

We thus realized that a long time might pass before we, in whose fate not many victor nations were interested, would be able to go home. Shipping space for enemy prisoners was certainly not a priority for the Allies at that time. Consequently we prepared for many more months—if not years—of prison life.

However, this was hard to take. In fact, many of us felt that it was more difficult to cope with our way of life after the end of the war than during it. For a while I found myself so listless that I had to force myself to carry out my self-imposed daily program of studying and writing. But eventually I got over it and settled down once more to the same rigorous program that had helped me to survive the more than five years that already lay behind me.

Another cause of tension was the uncertainty about our loved ones. I had heard from time to time from my mother during the war years. The last letter received from her before the Russian spring offensive cut Berlin off from the outside world was dated December 9, 1944. It arrived June 8, 1945. Under the date of April 25 our newspaper announced that the Russian Army was fighting its way into the heart of Berlin and was advancing along Prenzlauer Allee, the very street on which my mother lived. In one of her last letters she had written me that she would remain in the city whatever might come. Therefore I wondered whether she had survived Berlin's siege, bombardment, and capture.

I had not heard from my wife Jeanne for more than three and a half years. The last card I had received from her was dated January 9, 1942. She had admonished me to remain true to her and hold on to our faith and pledged to do the same. From week to week we waited for some news from our loved ones after the Japanese surrendered and the first Allied forces landed on Java. Finally the first letters from the East Indies arrived, but I was not yet among the lucky recipients.

But then on November 20, 1945, a letter from my wife reached me at last. Jeanne wrote that she had just heard through the Red Cross that I was still alive. Since for nearly four years she had considered herself to be a widow the news was as much a shock as a surprise. In a long letter she described what she had done during the last four and a half years. She had been able to continue her work as a nurse and had given Bible studies to several people, bringing nine of them into the church. Also she had undergone an appendectomy with the surgery performed by a Javanese doctor. Evidently she had come through the trying years of the war in good shape physically and mentally.

However, she also presented me with a long list of fellow workers who had died in Japanese prison camps: Hendrik Twynstra, whose assistant I had been during the first two years of my work in Djakarta; Louis M. D. Wortman, the principal of our training school, my closest friend among all the foreign missionaries; Marie Tilstra, the wife of the president of the Netherlands East Indies Union Mission, leaving three children behind, with the whereabouts of her husband not yet known (he turned up later in a Japanese POW camp in Burma); G. A. and A. Wood, a retired missionary couple from Australia who were still working in Sumatra when the war broke out; and M. R. Van Emmerik, a teacher in our training school. I could not help crying when I read this long list of friends and colleagues who had made the supreme sacrifice in a country to which they had dedicated their lives.

Another 16 months had to pass before I could embrace Jeanne once more. Six months after my arrival in America she reached Los Angeles, exactly on my birthday in the spring of 1947 and nearly seven years after we had said goodbye to each other in a police station in Djakarta. It was the best birthday gift I had ever received.

August 12, 1946, was another day of great rejoicing for me when it brought a letter from my mother. Now, more than a year after that war had ended, I learned from her that she had survived the baptism by fire and terror that all citizens of Berlin had passed through before, during, and after its conquest by the Soviet Army. Her letter also contained the good news that with the exception of an uncle and two cousins all my close relatives were still alive, including my brother and sister and their families, although some of them were POWs somewhere in Allied camps.

In the meantime we Adventist missionaries worked incessantly to regain our freedom. We were quite sure that we had little chance of returning to the East Indies in the foreseeable future, because of the strong anti-German feelings among the Dutch who were attempting to re-establish their control over their former colonial empire. Thus we made no efforts in that direction.

Instead, we offered our services to the Southern Asia Division and told the officers there that we would be willing to work as missionaries in any of the countries that belonged to the large division. They accepted our offer and contacted the General Conference headquarters in Washington, D.C., about it. The church leaders there consequently voted to transfer us from the control of the Far Eastern Division to the Southern Asia Division and made budgets available for our salaries. The division officers in Poona petitioned the Indian government to release us from custody and permit us to be employed as missionaries. The effort failed. The spokesman of the Home Department of the government of India declared that the time might come when interned Germans who had worked in India before the war might be allowed to remain in the country and resume their former activities, but not those who had never lived there before.

Our friends in the division then began to seek permission for us to go to America, since we had all worked for a mission board that had its headquarters in the United States. But this also posed problems. The Indian government refused to enter into any negotiations in regard to our status, saying they were only custodians of the German prisoners. The Dutch government had arrested them and transferred them to the country, and therefore the Dutch government should decide what it wanted to do with them.

New petitions had to be submitted, this time to the Dutch government, requesting it to allow the Indian government to release the German internees. Weeks passed before authorities in Holland reached a decision. Finally, back came the reply that the Indian government could free us if it felt inclined to do so. One obstacle had successfully been put out of the way. New ones waited in the wings.

In the meantime it had become summer 1946. All division officers had left for the United States to attend the General Conference session that convened in Washington D.C. The task of negotiating with the American consulate general and the Indian government had fallen on the shoulders of the assistant secretary-treasurer of the division, Mr. C. A. Hart, an Anglo-Indian, who carried out his task in a most efficient way. Looking back on the weeks when Mr. Hart commuted between the American consulate in Calcutta, which covered the northern part of India in which we were located, the Indian government offices in New Delhi, and our camp in Dehra Dun, it is incredible that a man who had also to carry out his regular work for the church, would show so much interest in our fate as he selflessly did, without expecting any special reward.

First he tried to find out whether the U.S. consul general would issue visas for us. The American consulate office informed him that it could authorize visas only to free citizens, not to prisoners. So Hart went to New Delhi armed with the reply of the Dutch government to his petition, which left to the Indian government the decision to free us or keep us in custody. In New Delhi he received word that the Indian government would release Germans if they had American visas and confirmed transportation to the United States. He had reached a stalemate. The Americans were not willing to grant visas to us as long as we were still prisoners, and the British were not willing to release us as long as we had no visas.

Since the matter of transportation was also involved, Hart had to act fast, because a large ocean liner, the S.S. *General Gordon,* was approaching Bombay. It was the first passenger ship made available after the war by the American military authorities to pick up the hundreds of American citizens who had been waiting for many months and years to return to their homeland. Mr. Hart had already purchased tickets for us on the S.S. *General Gordon* after having received the green light from the General Conference to do so.

In the meantime the American consulates in Calcutta and Bombay had agreed to let the Bombay office handle all business that pertained to passengers for the S.S. *General Gordon,* regardless of whether they came from the north or south of India, since the ship would dock in Bombay. That helped our case tremendously, for Mr. Hart was personally acquainted with the U.S. consul general in Bombay. Since the division office in Poona lay much closer to Bombay than to Calcutta (the latter being separated from Bombay by a continent) he had had frequent dealings with them over the years. When Hart learned that Bombay would handle all *General Gordon* passengers, he went at once to the U.S. consul general in that city and pleaded with him to help solve the problem.

The American official made a suggestion that in the end led to success. He expressed himself as willing to state in writing that he would issue us visas if we would present ourselves to his office as free men. Armed with this statement Hart traveled once more to New Delhi and presented the letter and the tickets to the Home Department, stressing the fact that the *General Gordon* would arrive in four days and sail for America in about a week. Any action required the utmost haste. After all we were still a two-day train ride from Bombay.

To make a long story short, the Delhi authorities showed themselves friendly toward Hart's pleading. When he left their office he carried with him an order to the commandant of the Dehra Dun camp to send us under escort to Bombay. There an official of the Home Department would release us into the custody of Mr. Hart, who would be responsible to see that we left the country on the S.S. *General Gordon*.

Since there was not time enough to send the order by mail, the Indian authorities allowed Hart to carry it himself. He took the next train to Dehra Dun where he arrived on Thursday morning, August 15. At once he called H. T. Terry, the principal of the Vincent Hill College, an Adventist academy at Mussoorie, to come and accompany him to the office of the commandant. Hart wanted to have some moral support in his dealings with the British colonel. During earlier visits the colonel had impressed Hart as a stern man, holding himself somewhat aloof from subordinates and civilians. Together Hart and Terry drove to the camp and presented themselves to the commandant's office.

Admitted into the official's presence, Hart presented to him the release document issued by the Home Department in New Delhi. It was quite evident that the administrator was not pleased to receive his orders in such an irregular way. It probably had never happened before that his superiors had used a civilian courier to bring his orders to him in person. He read the document and told Hart and Terry that he would naturally do what he was ordered to do, but that it would take days. His regulations required that any prisoner to be released had to be processed in the regular way. He had to have a physical examination by the camp doctor, had to get a battery of shots, had to have his camp money changed to normal Indian money, had to have all his written materials and books cleared by the censor, and, the colonel added, "Since these men came to this country without any passports or identification papers, we have to provide them with some kind of travel papers, which takes time." After a pause he added, "I doubt that you could even find seats on the trains to Bombay in time to get them there, since those trains are always sold out for several days in advance. You see, gentlemen, there is no way to get these 11 men to Bombay in time to catch the ship next Thursday."

Hart with all his persuasive power talked to the colonel, explaining to him how long he had worked on the case, how many trips he had made to Calcutta, to Simla where the Dutch ambassador had his residence, to Bombay, to Delhi, and to this camp, that he had finally succeeded in obtaining our release, visas, and a ship. Should all such success be lost because of procedural guidelines?

The commandant remained silent. Human feelings seemed to well up inside him. Suddenly he said, "I will see what I can do for you!" Then he picked up the phone, dialed the railroad station, and asked whether he could have 11 spaces on the Friday night train to Bombay. The railroad agent told him that he could have five spaces on Friday night and another six spaces on Sunday night. Nothing earlier was available. The commandant at once accepted.

Then he pressed one button after another on his desk, which

brought several officers to his office. He ordered the first one to have all Adventists brought to the visitors' room from the three wings in which they were housed. The next officer was to have the first five of us seen by the doctor that same afternoon to get our physical examinations and required injections and health certificates, and the other six the next morning. The third officer was to contact the censor's office to have examined at once all our books and written material we wanted to take with us, so they could accompany us when we left the camp. The fourth officer would direct the business office to change our camp money into Indian rupees and issue vouchers, with which he should purchase the railway tickets for the spaces he, the commandant, had already reserved for us, as well as tickets for two accompanying soldiers. Still another officer would have identification papers prepared for each one of us, while finally one officer would make the personnel arrangements for both our groups. Each would be accompanied by one armed guard who would travel inconspicuously in a lower class railway carriage so that the other passengers would not even know that we were under guard.

After having issued all the orders in the presence of his two visitors, the colonel dismissed them with the friendly words "Well, gentlemen, you have witnessed that I fully cooperated with your requests. If your friends don't reach their ship on time it is not my fault." Hart and Terry expressed their sincere thanks and left his office. From there they walked over to the small building that served as visitors' room.

In the meantime we had all been called and under the escort of our British wing commanders were taken to the visitors' room. None of us knew who had come to see us this time, although we hoped that it would be Mr. Hart carrying some good news for us since we knew how feverishly he was working on our behalf. Eventually we saw Hart and Terry emerging from the commandant's office.

After they had greeted each one of us, Mr. Hart announced, "Brethren, you are all released. Five of you will leave for Bombay tomorrow night, the other six Sunday night." For a minute or so, we stood in complete silence. Not even a thank-you came from our lips. The news had overwhelmed us. How long had we waited for this? Was this really true? So many times we had hoped and prayed about becoming free men again and being reunited with our loved ones, and how many times had we been disappointed? As I stared speechless at Hart he seemed to me like the angel who had appeared to Peter in a Jerusalem prison and bid him to get dressed, put his shoes on, and follow him into freedom (Acts 12:7,8).

As soon as we had regained our voices we profusely thanked Mr. Hart for all that he had done for us and bombarded him with questions about how he had accomplished what only a few days before had seemed a lost cause. After he told us the whole story, all of us unashamedly knelt down and, in the presence of the three British officers, poured out our hearts in gratitude to God for this wonderful experience.

When we returned to our respective wings and the news of our release had spread, we became "signs and wonders" among the men—to use the biblical expression of Isaiah 8:18. While now and then a single man had been released since the war had ended, we were the first group to regain its freedom among the thousands of internees. People were baffled. It seemed incredible that neither the powerful Roman Catholic Church nor any of the large Protestant denominations had so far successfully obtained the release of their priests, monks, or clergymen, while the small, insignificant Seventh-day Adventist Church managed to pull all their men out.

One person congratulated me and said, "God must like you Adventists very much. Not only are you the first to get away from this life, but you are going to America, the wealthiest land in the world. When the hour of freedom comes for us, we will be forced to return to a homeland whose cities have been destroyed, and which is humiliated and enslaved by the victorious powers. It may even be that we are better off here in this prison camp than free in Germany."

Since I belonged to the second group that would depart Sunday night, I had a little more time than those scheduled for Friday night. Hence we four Adventists in our wing could spend another Sabbath in camp. We used it for a long thanksgiving service in which we reviewed God's dealings with us during the past six and a half years of internment.

And then on Sunday afternoon we left the camp. A hand-drawn cart waited to take our suitcases and boxes to the main gate of the camp. Some of our friends had requested permission to bring our stuff to the gate and load it onto the army truck parked there. After having said goodbye to the hundreds of fellow internees in our wing we had to pass several other wings, and hundreds of others lined up to wish us Godspeed. Some of our acquaintances reached through the fence to shake our hands once more.

As I saw all those men standing there my eyes began to moisten. "When will the hour of freedom come for them?" I asked myself. "What will their future be? How many of them will find friendly hands stretched out to them to begin a new life, as our mission board is doing to us?" With all the joy that filled my heart for what God had done for us, I felt sorry for all those men who faced such a dark future.

At the main gate we took seats on top of our luggage and rode through the streets of Dehra Dun to the railway station. Arriving there we met several teachers from the school in Mussoorie who had come down from their mountaintop town to say goodbye to us. There was also our "angel," Mr. Hart, who had been forced to stay at the school in Mussoorie for three days because he had been unable to get an earlier seat on a train back to Bombay.

The delay in his travel plans was almost providential, because we found out the next morning that we badly needed his assistance in Delhi. Our train from Dehra Dun ran late and reached the Delhi railway station a few minutes after the departure time of the Frontier Mail, the Bombay express train. When we pulled into the station we saw that our connecting train still stood on its track. Mr. Hart leaped out of our train and raced up the stairs of the overpass and down the other side to reach the other track. As the stationmaster stood there, ready to give the sign to the engineer to depart, he saw Hart running down the steps. He called out, "Get in fast, the train is leaving!" But Mr. Hart rushed to him and pleaded with him to let the train wait a few minutes to let us six passengers of the *General Gordon* on board since we might otherwise miss the ship's departure time. The stationmaster acceded to his request. Quickly Hart took several porters and got all our luggage transferred from the luggage car of the train on which we had arrived to the Frontier Mail. In the meantime we had found our reserved spaces, took Mr. Hart in, and the train left several minutes behind time. Another crisis had passed.

When we reached Bombay on Tuesday night we saw for the first time our "shadow," the armed soldier who had traveled with us in another part of the train. At the Bombay railway station we also met an official from the Home Department who gave to the soldier a written receipt for the delivery of six internees, which he had to take back to the Dehra Dun camp commandant. Then he handed us over to Mr. Hart. Now we were really free and could go wherever we wanted—an indescribably wonderful feeling that only those who have passed through a similar experience can fully appreciate.

Wednesday was the only day we had in Bombay before our departure. The most important errand for us was to visit the American consulate and obtain our visitor's visas to the United States.

The remainder of the day passed in a blur of activity. We received money from Mr. Hart and made some necessary purchases. We also wrote letters. I notified Jeanne that I was free and on my way to America where I hoped soon to be reunited with her. And I mailed one to my mother, who had lived in Berlin through hundreds of bombing raids, the capture of the city by the Russian Army, and the famine conditions after the war. Now I wanted her to know the good news of my release as soon as possible and promised to send her Care packages when I reached America.

That evening the Bombay Adventist Church feted the 11 of us like heroes, and we gave our testimony. It was a marvelous experience to be again in a church building for a worship service with fellow believers in the Adventist faith, a privilege denied us for six and a half years.

Chapter VIII

Epilogue

Our four-week voyage on the S.S. *General Gordon* was enjoyable and on the whole uneventful. It took us from Bombay via Singapore, Manila, and Hong Kong to San Francisco. Although we stopped in Singapore only four hours, it was long enough to let some journalists become aware of our presence. "Eleven Nazis on Board the S.S. *General Gordon,*" the headlines of a newspaper announced the next morning.

In Manila, where our ship stopped for two days, we went ashore. There we met our missionaries who were busy reorganizing the church work and rebuilding destroyed institutions. Also we saw for the first time a large city almost completely devastated. Although a year had passed since the Asiatic war had ended, the streets of Manila were still filled with the debris of thousands of collapsed buildings, shot-up tanks and army trucks, burned-out streetcars, and other vehicles. The only visible traffic was carried on by military jeeps. An emergency power plant towed from the United States across the Pacific and stationed on a gigantic barge in the harbor provided the city's electricity. The water was still not safe to drink without being boiled, and in Manila Bay lay scores of sunken ships, their masts or funnels sticking out of the water.

Our stay in Hong Kong also lasted two days. Since the authorities would not permit us to go ashore, our fellow missionaries from America came to us on board and told us of the conditions through which they had passed during the war, and what they had found when they had returned to their work in China.

Finally came our glorious arrival in San Francisco on Wednesday, September 18, 1946. Some passengers who knew San Francisco had told me that although the city lay in a picturesque spot on California's central coast, I should not expect too much. In fact, they warned me that we should encounter a morning fog at that time of the year. It could even prevent us from seeing the Golden Gate Bridge—then the longest suspension bridge on earth—when we would sail underneath it and enter San Francisco Bay.

The opposite was true. I arose early on the day of our arrival, since I did not want to miss the entrance into the bay. Coming on deck, I found that we had a cloudless sky. The Golden Gate Bridge presented itself in all its grandeur, as did the hills surrounding the bay. The hilly city of San Francisco with its highrise buildings in the downtown area lay before me in all its beauty, some of it fashioned by nature, the rest by the ingenuity of men. I fell instantly in love with San Francisco, a love that never left me and influenced me 30 years later to choose one of its suburbs as the place to spend my retirement years.

My reunion with Jeanne finally took place on my birthday in Los Angeles in the spring of 1947. After the glorious day of my own release, it was the most happy day I had experienced in a long time. Six years later I saw my mother again in Berlin, 21 years after I had said goodbye to her there.

Many busy and happy years followed my arrival as a free man in the United States. First I spent four and a half years obtaining the necessary degrees so that I could teach the subjects in which I was more interested than in any other: biblical archaeology and Old Testament history. Then I taught for 26 years at Andrews University Theological Seminary and at extension schools on four continents, wrote hundreds of articles, published several books, edited a learned journal for 12 years, took part in and directed archaeological expeditions in Palestine, and founded the archaeological museum that now bears my name.

Standing in the evening shadows of my life and looking back, I cherish not only my years as a teacher and scholar but also the years that prepared me for my life's task, including the six and a half years I was forced to spend in five prison camps. Without them I could not have written the preceding paragraph. I can honestly say that I am now as grateful for those apparently long, lost years as I am for the many beautiful ones that followed them. I definitely have experienced in my own life the truth of the claim of the apostle Paul "that all things work together for good to them that love God"

(Rom. 8:28), as well as the statement of another inspired writer: "God never leads His children otherwise than they would choose to be led, if they could see the end from the beginning, and discern the glory of the purpose which they are fulfilling" (*The Desire of Ages*, pp. 224,225).